UN/MASKED

UN/MASKED

MEMOIRS OF A GUERRILLA GIRL ON TOUR

DONNA KAZ

AKA APHRA BEHN

Skyhorse Publishing

Skyhorse Publishing books may be purchased in bulk at special discounts for sales promotion, corporate gifts, fund-raising, or educational purposes. Special editions can also be created to specifications. For details, contact the Special Sales Department, Skyhorse Publishing, 307 West 36th Street, 11th Floor, New York, NY 10018 or info@skyhorsepublishing.com.

Skyhorse® and Skyhorse Publishing® are registered trademarks of Skyhorse Publishing, Inc.®, a Delaware corporation.

Visit our website at www.skyhorsepublishing.com.

10 9 8 7 6 5 4 3 2 1

Library of Congress Cataloging-in-Publication Data is available on file.

Cover design by Laura Klynstra
Cover photo: Lyn Hughes

Print ISBN: 978-1-5107-0943-0
Ebook ISBN: 978-1-5107-0945-4

Printed in the United States of America

For Richard Charkham

Beyond the mountain is another mountain.
—Haitian proverb

Nothing's impossible I have found,
For when my chin is on the ground
I pick myself up, dust myself off,
Start all over again.
—Dorothy Fields, *Pick Yourself Up*

CONTENTS

Photo by Lyn Hughes

UN/MASKED

1

MASKED

As a child I felt powerful. A faint but steady motor fluttered inside my rib cage, lifting my raw and fearless soul with every fanciful step I took. I was smart. I was beautiful. I was second-generation Polish-American. I could do anything. These characteristics would catapult me directly into an amazing adult life.

I would have gotten there had I not moved to New York City in the fall of 1977 and walked south down Fifth Avenue to Greenwich Village to look for work. I would have gotten there if the manager at Jimmy Day's Bar and Restaurant on West 4th Street and Barrow had not hired me on the spot. I would have gotten there if the actor who worked at the theatre around the corner had not decided to have lunch at Jimmy Day's my first week on the job.

For a long time I have attempted to rewind my narrative back to the confident young woman whose life lay before her. I have put my hands on her memory, pried it open, groped around and around to catch hold of who she was. I need her back. The artist on the brink cannot see the danger ahead. I want to tell her how precious is her talent. I want to tell her danger never looks like danger until it is too late. Her original, primal force is not to be given away.

I cannot do any of that. All I can do is take the rubber gorilla mask from the dressing room table and slip it over my head. All I can do is make my way to the wings and wait for my cue. All I can do is run onstage and grunt and growl and pound my chest until the audience laughs and claps and hollers and finally weeps when they understand I am here to tell them there are women all over the world who have been kept from living the lives they were born to, like me.

2

NEW YORK CITY

1977: A RENTED U-HAUL TRAILER HITCHED to the rear of my brother Ken's Oldsmobile contains all of my possessions. Both car and trailer barely fit onto the narrow roadway of the 59th Street Bridge. We are headed for Manhattan. I am moving from Long Island to New York City to be an actress. Each time the trailer grinds against the side railing I think of the young, strong, smart, and funny female characters in brand-new plays I will soon have the chance to portray onstage.

Scrape! A pirate. *Scrape!* An Olympian. *Scrape!* A scientist.

My possessions barely fill the small bedroom in the big loft I have rented with two other women on the corner of 19th Street and Fifth Avenue. I use the near-empty fifteen hundred square feet to rehearse one-minute audition monologues and sixteen-bar songs.

I rise at dawn to attend open calls and appointments. I read pages from new plays, do my best to interpret vapid teenagers, despondent servants, and oversexed prostitutes with panache. Where are the smart female roles? I want to ask the men writing these plays, *How about writing the part of a woman pirate with good leadership skills?* I do not audition for a single character I would actually like to portray.

1982: I become a playwright.

My beloved friend and creative partner, Charles T. Harper, takes poems and journal entries I have written over the past ten years and together we shape them into my first play, which he directs and stages in the parlor of his spacious Upper West Side apartment. We cast the best actors we know and invite all our friends. It is a particular and personal artistic success. Soon afterwards I begin a new full-length play.

My new full-length play is picked up by a producer who invests in a workshop production. Charles directs. I use the play as a writing sample and receive a coveted invitation to the artists' colony Yaddo to develop it. While I began writing plays for myself to act in, I soon lose the desire. I am content being just a playwright.

To earn a living I wait tables in a brand-new, cavernous restaurant across from Lincoln Center. Everyone who waits tables here, or most likely anywhere in New York for that matter, is really an artist: an actor or a writer or a dancer or a singer. Artists are good waiters because both jobs require some of the same skills. You have to have energy and passion. You have to be a fast thinker, be able to improvise. You have to use your imagination to invent descriptions of food you have never tasted and wines you have never sipped. You have to pretend there is no place you would rather be and nothing you would rather be doing than scribbling down, on a grease-stained dupe pad, precisely how someone wants their burger cooked.

At 7 p.m., an hour before every single person seated in my section has to have a glass or two of cheap wine, finish their this-is-much-too-big-for-one-person entrée, drink a cup of thin coffee, and split a gooey dessert, my muscles tingle with the anticipation and eagerness of an opening night. I will make sure every one of my customers has an entertaining experience akin to the other show they will soon see at Lincoln Center. Waiting on tables is giving the performance of my career, table after table, night after night.

So why go home after my shift is through for a good night's sleep in order to rise early to write the next day? My artistic aspirations are spent and satisfied during my wait shift. A quick drink at the bar to unwind turns into two, then three. I get home later and later. On some nights I stay until the sun comes up, head home to crash for a few hours before I rise and repeat the pattern over and over again.

1986: My writing slows and stalls. Just when it seems I am going to be gobbled up by my routine and wait tables forever, the producer who picked up my first full-length play offers me a job with her film development company. I start as a script reader, writing detailed analysis, called coverage, of what potential, if any, newly published novels have to be made into feature films. When the company produces their first movie I am sent on location to Philadelphia and thrown onto the crew as an assistant director. I love this new work, and so when the company closes their New York office and offers me a position in their Los Angeles branch, I accept.

It takes me only a few months to understand that Los Angeles and the film business is a misogynistic twilight zone.

PRODUCER: What are we shooting?

ME: The part where JANE DOE discovers radioactivity.

PRODUCER: What's she wearing in that?

ME: A lab coat.

PRODUCER: Change it to a black leather catsuit.

I exaggerate (but not by much).

In Los Angeles I am pulled back into writing for the theatre by understanding I will probably not find a welcoming place in film. I am in my thirties and already considered ancient. I have no interest in writing for the screen because movies about interesting women are rarely made. The production crew of the first film I worked on employed only a handful of women. I must return to my first love, the theatre, and its parity, equal opportunity, and diversity. I crack open a fresh notebook and go back to writing plays.

1994: After eight years in film and television, I wake up, get in my car, drive to LAX, and board a plane back to New York City. Get me the hell out of here, I whisper to the flight attendant who scans my ticket. Somewhere over Milwaukee, as I sip from a minibottle of

Chardonnay, I fantasize that my return to New York City theatre will finally rid my life of sexism in the arts forever.

My first day back in Manhattan I pick up the *New York Times* to find out what is playing around town. Why, plays by men are playing around town . . . plays by white men. Almost all of the plays being produced in New York City are written by white men, directed by white men, designed by white men, and the artistic directors of the companies I aim to send my scripts to are also white men. The current theatre scene is overwhelmingly dominated and therefore controlled by white men, which can only mean one thing: no matter how good my plays are, they will never see the light of day unless I am a man.

Perhaps LA was not so bad after all.

I ignore the sad statistics about New York City theatre and dutifully submit my scripts to theatres for development. I quickly find myself a New York City playwright stuck in development hell. My plays are read and revised, read and revised, read and revised over and over, again and again.

> LIGHTS UP on Producer's Office, 1501 Broadway, New York City.
>
> PRODUCER (male) and PLAYWRIGHT (female) are in the middle of a meeting.

PRODUCER
Loved your script. Let's do a reading of it!

BLACKOUT

> LIGHTS UP on Producer's Office, the following month.

PLAYWRIGHT

I learned so much from that reading. Here's my second draft.

PRODUCER

Great! Let's do a reading of it.

BLACKOUT

LIGHTS UP on Producer's Office,
the following month.

PLAYWRIGHT

I learned so much from the second reading. Here's my third
draft.

PRODUCER

Great! Let's do a reading of it.

BLACKOUT

LIGHTS UP on Producer's Office,
the following month.

PLAYWRIGHT

I learned so much from the third reading. Here's my fourth
draft.

PRODUCER

Great! Let's do a reading of it!

PLAYWRIGHT goes to WINDOW.
Opens it. Climbs out as LIGHTS
FADE.

It began to sink in. I am not

     the right

         gender.

What to do? Return to LA. Become a man. Tackle sexism in theatre. I discard the easiest choice, the hardest choice, and lunge for the most righteous. People just do not realize what is happening, I think. When everyone is hip to how sexist Broadway and off-Broadway is, they will not buy tickets. If people do not buy tickets, the theatre will collapse. Producers will have no choice but to produce plays by women. There is a tragedy on Broadway and it isn't *Electra*, and, by golly, I am going to make sure people know about it!

Around this time the Dramatists Guild, a national advocacy organization, announces a panel discussion for women playwrights. Perhaps I can start my campaign for women playwrights there. I enthusiastically show up.

    — Oh, just ignore all those producers and produce your own plays yourself! Stop whining and waiting for someone else to put your play on. It's that simple!

    The woman on the Dramatists Guild panel is flipping her heels up and down on the carpet under the table, practically kicking in glee, proud of her gumption and ability to coax a shitload of cash donations from family and friends to self-produce her plays. I raise my hand.

    — There is nothing wrong with producing your own plays, I say, but why is self-production the only alternative? Why aren't plays by women produced?

    I hear faint mumbles of agreement come from several other women in the room. Then another playwright stands up and asks if perhaps the problem is discrimination.

The woman on the panel gulps.

— Did you just say dis-crim-in-a-tion!? Why, it's the nineties, for gosh sake!

I rip my copy of the *New York Times* out of my bag and open it to the theatre listings.

— Look at the listings. There is just one play by a woman in the entire lot. If that's not discrimination, what is it?

— Good point, a woman playwright to my right whispers.

— Things will never change until we find out why plays by women are not produced, says another.

A few of us linger when the meeting is over. One of them, playwright Anne Harris, proposes that we continue the discussion. The director of special events at the Guild agrees and puts us on the calendar. The following month we facilitate a meeting at the Guild called "Producing Plays by Women," which begins as a quiet sharing of statistics and quickly dissolves into a strident bitch fest. For ninety minutes women playwrights stand up and share their stories of being kept out of the white boys' club that is theatre, culminating in a collective cry: WHERE ARE THE WOMEN?

> LIGHTS UP on ARTISTIC DIRECTOR standing center stage in front of the curtain before a show. He addresses the audience.

ARTISTIC DIRECTOR

Finally, we are pleased to announce that the theme of this year's Every-Seventh-Tuesday-Night reading series in our black box/off-off-off Broadway space located in the abandoned smallpox hospital on Roosevelt Island will be Worthy New Works by Emerging Women. The first play to be read will be a drama by Agatha Christie.

This memoir is interrupted by a woman on hold to Telecharge.

WOMAN ON HOLD TO TELECHARGE

Please! I really don't care about women in theatre, I just want to see a good show! Besides, this issue does not affect me. There are so many much more important issues that need my support. People are starving. Violence is rampant. The climate is out of control. Stop complaining that your own plays are not being produced.

ME

It's not about my plays, it's about the fact that there are no women's voices in mainstream theatre and those voices should be heard. The lack of equality affects everything from world hunger to war. Without the vision of women and artists of color the theatre is like a play without a second act!

WOMAN ON HOLD TO TELECHARGE

If you think I'm going to pay for premium seats to see just one act, think again!

ME

Exactly my point.

End of interruption.

1995: I am awarded the Quidel Corporation fellowship residency at the artist's colony Djerassi in Woodside, California. Back on the West Coast, I spend the month of August working on a brand-new play in a private studio overlooking acres of secluded land next to Neil Young's cattle ranch along with two other writers, two performance artists, a composer, and a visual artist.

At the first communal dinner I sit across from the visual artist, a woman from New York City. Between forkfuls of rice pilaf and sips of red wine, we discuss our work and the current state of women in the arts. As we compare notes, we agree that both the theatre and the art world are blatantly sexist. Sensing my smoldering rage as I recite the lack of women being produced on Broadway and beyond, she reaches into her bag and pulls out the newly published *Confessions of the Guerrilla Girls*.

— Read this, she commands.

— What is it?

— Just read it. I will talk to you about it when you're done.

That night I pace the floor of my studio and devour every page of *Confessions of the Guerrilla Girls*. I get it. I so get it. I hear the message as if a hot mouth screams it dangerously close to my ear— sexism is alive and well and living in the art world, shout the Guerrilla Girls.

The gorilla-mask-wearing, miniskirted, high-heeled, and totally badass Guerrilla Girls: a group of women artists who funnel their outrage at discrimination in museums and galleries into the creation of deft black-and-white posters that humorously state the sorry statistics surrounding women artists: over 80 percent of the nudes in the paintings in the Met Museum are of women, but only 3 percent were painted by women. The Guerrilla Girls conclude by asking if, in order to get into the Met, women have to be naked.

The Guerrilla Girls wheat-paste their posters all over SoHo in the dead of night, slapping up posters on construction fences, postboxes, and lampposts. They call themselves Eva Hesse,[1] Rosalba

---

1 Eva Hesse (1936–1970), sculptor and painter. Pioneered work in plastics, latex, and fiberglass.

Carriera,[2] Djuna Barnes,[3] Lyubov Popova,[4] and other names that are not their own but those of dead women artists who have struggled and created before them. They do this to avoid being accused of carrying out their actions to promote and float their own careers as artists. Their posters are funny and poignant and force you to rethink what you know about women artists and sexism. Soon everyone wants to know who they really are.

I was told that for their first press conference a member was sent out to buy guerrilla disguises to cover their faces. This particular Guerrilla Girl was a very bad speller and came back with gorilla masks instead. The mistake turned out to be the perfect look. With black rubber gorilla masks over their heads, the Guerrilla Girls instantly turned themselves into modern masked avengers in the tradition of the Lone Ranger, Zorro, and Catwoman.

Well into the night I read and reread *Confessions of the Guerrilla Girls*. I envision an attack on sexism in the theatre world lurking in the text for every poster about sexism in the art world. What a coup it would be to name the theatres that do not produce women playwrights or plays by writers of color. How cool to prove bus companies are more inclusive in their hiring practices than theatres are. Finally, the word would be out and theatres would no longer discriminate against women and minority artists.

On the last page of the book are instructions: How to be a Guerrilla Girl. Yes! Wait. No. Alas, one cannot just up and join the Girls. But there are further instructions. Readers should steal the Girls' ideas, make posters, and form their own groups. Already there are Guerrilla

---

2 Rosalba Carriera (1673–1757), Venetian rococo painter. Popularized use of pastels for portraits.

3 Djuna Barnes (1892–1982), writer of influential works of modernist literature. Author of *Nightwood*.

4 Lyubov Popova (1889–1924), Russian avant-garde painter, graphic artist, textile designer, and art theorist.

Girls groups from Pennsylvania to Paris. My spirit lifts and I am buoyant with the hope I might have stumbled on a way to end sexism in the American theatre.

The next morning on the way to breakfast, I ambush my new visual artist friend at Djerassi. I explain to her the Guerrilla Girls are exactly the kind of activist intervention the theatre world needs. I open *Confessions of the Guerrilla Girls* and blabber on and on about how the tactics of the Girls might be used to attack the theatre world. Then I ask her if she happens to know any Guerrilla Girls.

She lowers her eyes and looks around.

— What? Do you know who they are? You must put me in touch with them!

— Shhhhhh. Not so loud!

My new artist friend pulls me off the path and scans the barbed-wire fence for anyone who might be close enough to eavesdrop on our conversation. We are surrounded by nothing but cows. Convinced the coast is clear, she leans her face in to mine and with a minty exhale whispers:

— Yes, I do. You're looking at one.

How I Became a Guerrilla Girl
A short play

> LIGHTS UP: Two women on a dirt road surrounded by cattle. Neil Young's "Heart of Gold," sounding acoustic and live, plays in the background from an unknown source. The women, KAZ and POPOVA, are in the middle of a conversation. POPOVA is leaning in, whispering into KAZ's ear.

                        KAZ

(jerking her head back) WHAT?! Could you repeat what you just
said?

                       POPOVA

You can't tell anyone who I really am! Promise me you will never tell
a soul!

                        KAZ

I promise! I promise!

                              (POPOVA looks around. COWS
                              blink and chew cud.)

                       POPOVA

Would you like to be a Guerrilla Girl?

                        KAZ

Is the sky blue? Is the pope Catholic? Do vacuum cleaners suck?
WHEN CAN I START!?

                              (Dust flies as COWS begin to
                              STAMPEDE.)

                      BLACKOUT

Lyubov Popova is the Guerrilla Girl I meet at Djerassi. Lyubov Popova
promises to call me as soon as the Guerrilla Girls are accepting new
members but warns it might take a while. Lyubov Popova explains
that some of the Girls, like her, are burned out and want to retire, but
not before they make sure new and energetic members are added to the
group who can bounce the Girls into a future where when people talk
about art they also talk about gender parity. But, she admonishes, the

Guerrilla Girls are a collective of women artists with strong opinions and various different goals. Not all Guerrilla Girls are alike.

Renewed by the residency and ebullient with images of myself as a future-feminist masked avenger, I return to New York City and throw myself into my work. I begin to understand what I am trying to say as an artist. I weave together distinctive experiences with the erudition I have gathered in the course of my life as a woman. I feel a heightened connection to the human race, as if it is impossible to disengage from other human beings. This humanness is what makes me an artist. I begin to believe that being an artist means taking responsibility for the world I saunter, breathe, and create in. *Is there a difference, then, between being an artist and being an activist?* I ask myself. It is often a sense of oppression that prompts me to create. As an artist/activist I want to change the narrow, male-centered focus of the current theatre because I believe it is for the greater good.

ART + ACTION =

In the fall of 1996, Anne Harris and I write a letter to the executive director of the Dramatists Guild and ask him to put us on the agenda for the Guild's annual meeting. We want to talk about how we think the Guild might better advocate for its women members.

MEMO

The Dramatists Guild's annual meeting is closed to associate members. But there is a place to voice your concerns. The Guild has a women's committee.

Anne and I search and discover a member of the Guild's women's committee. She tells us that, sadly, the women's committee is inactive and has been for some time. We offer to help her reactivate it. With a few other women we form a steering committee and caucus outside the Guild. We ask the Guild to give us space to convene and to post a notice of the meetings in their newsletter. I fax the DG executive director to let him know I have found the women's committee and the dates we have selected as the first few meetings at the Guild.

MEMO

Only members of the Guild's governing council can sit on Guild committees. The women's committee was initially formed incorrectly.

I obtain a copy of the Guild's constitution. There is no reference anywhere stating who can and cannot sit on DG committees. Anne and I schedule a meeting with the DG executive director. We ask him for permission to present to the Guild's governing council a proposal to outline the limited scope of our renewed women's committee. We are confident the Guild will not object to a bunch of woman playwrights meeting once a month in their offices. The DG executive director tells us the steering committee is the proper group to present our proposal to. If we write it out he will deliver our proposal directly to them.

— Who sits on this steering committee?

— I cannot tell you. It is an anonymous committee.

— How many are on it?

— Seven.

— How many women?

— Half.

— Does that mean four or three?

— Thanks for stopping by.

DISPOSED OF

July 1997: Our ally on the women's committee gets a phone call from the DG executive director. The steering committee has unanimously voted against reactivating the women's committee. If we want to continue meeting as a separate organization we can rent space from them. We request that the Dramatists Guild publish this decision in the monthly newsletter.

MEMO

No.

The steering committee/women's committee continues to meet outside the Guild. Perhaps our focus is too narrow. We ditch the idea of the women's committee and work on a new idea for a committee to advocate on behalf of Guild members from all underrepresented groups. We bypass the DG executive director and write letters directly to every member of the Guild's council with our proposal. Tony Kushner responds. He thinks it is a great idea. We wait weeks for more responses. In the end, Kushner is the only council member who replies to our letter.

DISMISSED

The refusal to address the annual meeting.

The you-cannot-activate-a-committee-because-you-are-not-on-the-council rule.

The you are not allowed to meet with the council.

The we will not even tell you who the council is.

The unanimous vote no from the anonymous seven.

The denial to publish the final decision.

And every unanswered letter painstakingly crafted and addressed to the council melds and mixes with all the other pushbacks I have experienced, i.e., leers on the sidewalk; hisses from the shadows; books, songs, television programs, movies, and plays depicting women as sex-crazed sidekicks, virginal martyrs, or empty-headed bimbos.

I mean verbal putdowns and nonverbal putdowns and gropes on the subway and hands up my skirt as I try to take your dinner order, every little which way I am reminded there is not a chance in hell to make a difference because I am a woman and that means I am

— O

—— U

——— T

OUT!

All these dismissals add up fast and become the last straw, the match in the mythical bra-burning trash can, because as these recollections now tick by they pile up and gain momentum until they explode inside of me with the energy of a generation.

All right, Dramatists Guild! Two can play at this game! I'll show you! Watch this!!! My resignation will resound through the halls of the Guild like an automatic gong stuck on repeat.

    TO: Mr. Peter Stone: President, Dramatists Guild

    Dear Mr. Stone,

        I am resigning from the Guild effective 10/1/1997

    Sincerely,

    Donna Kaz

    CC: Terrence McNally, Vice President

    Arthur Kopit, Secretary

    Richard Lewine, Treasurer

    Tony Kushner

Boom!

    Boom!

        Boom?

I sign up for playwriting support groups organized by women. With other women playwrights I try to encourage everyone to press on. But

in my heart I fear each of us is buying into the message we are being sent by the theatre world: we are not producing your plays because they are not good enough. Rejection letters pile up in the mail: their contents swirl before my eyes.

> *We've decided we're not interested in your script.*
> *We have decided not to pursue a production of your play.*
> *Your play does not suit our needs or interest at this time.*
> *We have no place for your play.*
> *We're not interested.*

Sincerely,

The Literary Manager (or perhaps in reality Joshua P., the every other Monday from 1–2 p.m. Literary Intern/Volunteer/Student)

Then, in the fall of 1997, my phone rings.

— Hello?

— This is Gertrude Stein[5] calling.

— Excuse me?

— It's Gertrude Stein, Guerrilla Girl, on the line.

---

5 Gertrude Stein (1874–1946), American writer of novels, poetry, and plays.

3

1977, NEW YORK CITY

I DO NOT REALLY SEE HIM as he stands in the doorway of Jimmy Day's Bar and Restaurant on West 4th Street in Greenwich Village. Behind him the sun wraps the glass door and windows in gold. From my position, slouched against the end of the bar, all I see is the outlined silhouette of a tall man holding a briefcase. When the sun moves behind a cloud and the shimmering glass oozes clear to display the dull city street behind it, my eyes adjust and there he is, looking lost and helpless.

He is as perfect a man as I have ever laid eyes on. Tall, blond, handsome as a model, gorgeous as a goddamn god.

I push myself into an upright position and stand firmly on two feet. Music plunks from the jukebox in the corner. I feel pulled forward like a magnet; pushed from behind like a schoolgirl on a playground; jolted into consciousness like a sleepwalker in front of a minefield.

He is looking this way and that, unsure of what to do, politely waiting for someone to guide him. Then his eyes land on me.

— I've got this one, I say to my coworkers, Adrienne and Maureen, practically knocking them down as I bound straight for him.

— Take any table you like, I command, and then immediately turn and briskly walk away as if burgers are piling up under the heat lamps and the cook is ding, ding, dinging the pickup bell.

At Jimmy Day's no burgers sit under the heat lamps and the pickup bell is silent. The cook lounges in the hallway on an overturned plastic bucket, methodically peeling potatoes. The bartenders, Mel and Gino, chew on plastic stirrers and dry beer mugs. Adrienne and Maureen marry ketchup bottles at the end of the bar.

He sits at a two-top and lights a cigarette. I watch him dig through his briefcase and pull out a manuscript. He draws deeply on a Winston, blows the smoke out of the side of his mouth, and opens the script to the first page. As I approach the table he looks up just at the moment I pass. I circle back around and stop to the right of his shoulder. His head is still turned to the left, looking for where I have gone.

— Drink?

He twists his head around and stares up at me. He wears wire-rimmed glasses and has a curved scar on his cheek. His blond hair is fine and soft. His chiseled chin holds the slightest trace of a dimple. His lips are moist. His nose is faultless.

— You're new here, he says, more a statement than a question.

— Yes, I am.

— What do you do? Besides waitressing, I mean.

— I'm an actress.

— Theatre lifts the spirit of man. It inspires bold and noble thoughts. I congratulate you.

He holds out his hand, his palm open up to the sky. I feel my body pull away from the table. His features melt into a grin full of straight white teeth. I place my hand on top of his. My brow furrows as I feel his fingers gently wrap around my hand, one by one.

— I'll have a cheeseburger and a half carafe of white wine.

— What? Oh, sure.

I pull my hand away, smooth my forehead with my wrist, take out my dupe pad and pen, and pretend I am writing it down.

— Coming right up.

He eats his burger neatly and drains his half carafe quickly. We exchange a few words every time I swing by his table. When he leaves he asks me what my schedule is and promises to pop in the next time I am working.

In the weeks that follow I find out he is an actor. His name is Bill. He works at Circle Rep around the corner, an off-Broadway ensemble theatre company with a solid reputation for staging both new and classic plays. He is married, but in the process of separating from his wife.

What? I mean, I hope "separating" as in getting a divorce real soon and not as in trying to reconcile with her.

— You working things out with her?

— No. How about you?

— Me? I'm single. I mean, not married. There's no one, not one person who is special, I mean, right now in my life.

Stop talking. Play it cool.

On slow shifts I spend a few minutes at his table where we have brief, intense conversations. He is well-read and smart and seems genuinely interested in what I have to say. With his face close to mine, he murmurs heady concepts of art and life. His tobacco-scented words form a narcotic bubble and engulf me in his own captivating little world.

When I get off work I park myself at the bar and sip my free shift drink, a draft beer, while I banter back and forth with the bartenders. I keep an eye toward the big front windows and secretly hope he will walk by. If I think I spot him, my stomach lifts up into my lungs and my entire body freezes, only to release with a nervous laugh when I realize it is not him.

Sometimes he comes in with a group of Circle Rep cast members after a show. They sit at a big round table, drink our famous heavy pour cocktails, and scream laughter at each other over the jukebox music deep into the night. He introduces me around the table but no one ever remembers me when they come in again. He is always the last to leave, spends a few minutes just with me, hugs me tightly before he leaves.

— I want to see a play you're in, I tell him on a slow, muggy afternoon.

— Fine. When it's right I'll get you a ticket.

He holds me close, takes my hand and squeezes it as if to send me a secret signal, a signal that says, wait.

I do not have time to wait. I am an artist with a plan: move to New York City (check); get a job (check); join a theatre company/dance troupe and perform (unchecked). Obsessed with training, I take two, sometimes three modern dance classes a day, leaping across sprung wood floors to frenzied drumbeats until I am drenched in sweat. Inspired by the downtown theatre scene, I seek out experimental theatres and offer to sweep the floors of their offices in exchange for the chance to observe their work. New York City in 1977, with its feverish rhythm and glitzy grime, pops my eyeballs so far out I weep at art exhibits or in movies or just from looking out of the window of my eighth-floor loft at the crazy gorgeousness of it all. I have finally arrived and stand poised on the brink of a stunning career. The city is as desperate as I am, and so I inject myself with all the terrifying beauty it has to offer and drink until dawn; do every drug I can get my hands on; sleep with guys I did not go to college with.

In the middle of all this there he is, a part of my routine, present for almost every shift I work, a smile on his cherub lips, his eyes gazing straight into mine as he asks me what I think about everything.

Just before Thanksgiving I find him out on the sidewalk at dusk as I finish up my shift.

— I didn't want to come in.

— Why not?

— I wanted to wait until you were off. What are you doing now?

— Going home. Two early dance classes tomorrow.

— Can I walk you there?

— Sure.

We arrive at a building on West 19th Street, just off of Fifth Avenue.

— This is where I live, believe it or not. The elevator doesn't work on weekends because it's really a commercial building. There's a sweat-shop on every floor but the eighth. And no intercom. You have to call from the pay phone on the corner and wait for me to throw you down an envelope with the key in it to get in. Hear that pounding? That's a disco called the Inferno on the first floor. Every night my floor pulses with the grinding rhythms from Inferno's incredible sound system.

Awkward Pause.

— Well, good night. I'm going to start up. It's a long way to . . .

He does not hear me. Just as I turn he puts his arms around my waist and pulls me toward him, then skims his lips over mine. After a pause he jerks his head away to gaze into my eyes for a moment and then kisses me.

— Can I come up?

— No.

We kiss again. Then three more times before I shove him out the door and run up the stairs.

We will not have a one-night stand. I will not sleep with a married man. Both of our lives are bursting at the seams and are poised to col-lide brilliantly together. But it will not happen tonight. As I take the steps up two at a time, I know I have made an important decision. A mighty love lurks around my buzzing life and soon it will strike.

⚡

The fall passes. I see him almost every shift I work. The new year arrives. The spring comes and goes. He is there through it all, as reg-ular a customer as they come. Except he is the customer who sends me—down to the ladies' room to make sure my hair looks good—over to take an order so it appears I have no clue he just walked in—across to the bar to control my excitement because he just sat in my section. When our eyes meet I do my best not to run into his arms or let it show how elated I feel just to be in the same room with him.

In early June he strides into Jimmy Day's with a huge grin on his face. Something is different about this day, and I move toward him with intent. He lifts me with a bear hug and whispers in my ear.

— I got the lead in a big movie. And I moved out of my apartment.

When he returns me to my feet I am changed by possibility. I fumble, and can only think to extend my open palm and say, I congratulate you.

An envelope with my name on it waits for me behind the bar a few weeks later. Inside is a single ticket to a play with a note: "This is the one." The ticket is for *Fifth of July* by Lanford Wilson at Circle Rep that same night.

I finish my shift at four o'clock, walk home, shower, and carefully choose my outfit: jeans, sleeveless V-neck, cowboy boots. At seven o'clock I light up a joint, smoke half of it, and walk to the theatre.

The lights fade to black, the curtain goes up, and there he is as Ken Talley, a Vietnam vet, a homosexual, and a bilateral amputee.

Mother of holy shit can this guy act.

He is so natural, warm, kind, and sensitive on stage. His performance is a thread of energy woven into a taut line between us, the audience, and him, the actor. When an artist displays this much honesty right in front of you it is natural to be put into a trance, to sink into the velvet-covered seat, to grip the armrests and fall into a deep and innocent wonder. The rest of the cast are excellent. The play, astonishing. Bill is best of all.

After the last round of applause rings out I remain seated until the rest of the audience has left, excited and petrified of what lies ahead.

It happens to be his last performance. I meet him in the lobby, and along with the entire cast we head for a nearby bar. He asks me what I thought of the play. I open my mouth but nothing comes out. The cast laugh and joke and drink and swat him on the back and wish him good luck and leave. And then it is just the two of us.

⚡

One cowboy boot is on top of the desk, standing straight up, the heel holding down the cup of my new bra. A white button-down shirt, pair of loafers, one tube sock, red panties, jeans, a belt, and the other cowboy boot form a line from the door to my dresser. A half-full bottle of Molson Golden Ale with a cigarette butt floating inside is on the windowsill, pinning down the floral sheet my mom used to make the curtains covering the gated windows of my room. The smallest breeze puffs the curtain, but it is not enough to threaten the perch of the bottle.

I have just opened my eyes and take it all in, add up the inventory from the night before. I shift onto my back on the pullout sofa bed, twist a blanket tighter around my torso. A film of salt and moisture covers my skin.

I look up. Shirts and skirts on hangers dangle above my head. For a moment I am confused. Then I realize the sofa bed is not where it usually is. How did it get wedged up into my makeshift closet? I think for a split second and remember everything. I roll my head to the right.

He lies inches away on top of the blanket, looks straight at me and grins. His right hand reaches up and slowly moves the length of my arm until it meets my hand to lock it with his. We stay frozen like this for a minute; comfortable, relaxed, our shallow breaths matching. I am the first to speak.

— Bill.

— It's early. Why don't you go back to sleep?

— What time is it?

— Seven.

— When are you leaving?

— My flight isn't until tonight.

— Then we have all day.

— I would love that. But I have so many things I have to do before I go.

He does not leave my loft until two that afternoon. He is off to visit his father, who lives in Toledo, Spain. A much-needed vacation, he describes it. He would not have the chance to take a vacation for a very long time because he has just been cast in his first feature film, *Altered States*.

— It's based on a novel by Paddy Chayefsky. Know who he is?

— No.

— I will share his work with you. He's a great writer.

— Can we have something to eat first?

— *Marty*. Didn't you ever see *Marty*?

— Wasn't Ernest Borgnine in that?

— Yes. And *Network*!

— I think I have some eggs.

We talk and talk, a rambling conversation splintering off into many tangents. Sometimes he says something that reminds me of a song. I bolt to the stereo, flip through my LPs, and cue up the track. We stare out the window and listen for a time. That reminds him of a passage from a book and he pores over my stack of dog-eared paperbacks and stops to read aloud from something that reminds him of something else. In between bites of an American cheese omelet he orates the longest sentences I have ever heard.

— Borgnine found the true quiet space in the character of Marty by choosing the penultimate gesture of using his large paw of a hand to pat the back of his mother's frail fist, as if to soothe her, but the facticity of the gesture denotes a quelling of his ego and an appeasing of his instinctual desire to rebel against the forces which dictated his ultimate fate, a fate which is fixed, as it is fixed for all of us, and in some ways plucks us by the very hairs of our beards each and every day as it shocks us into taking our first breath the precise moment that we awaken.

— Fate is fixed, isn't it? But some of us don't have beards. More toast?

— I must go. I don't know if I can call you because my father lives in a very remote area. But I'll write. I promise, I will write you.

— You'd better take a lot of stationery with you.

— I'll be home in a few weeks.

— Here's my address.

— I'm coming back to you.

— Good.

⚡

Five days later a postcard arrives. Then another and another. On the front are photos of paintings by Spanish artists. On the other side, short messages. He is thinking about me.

I think about him too; at breakfast, in the subway, at work, on the phone. From the moment I open my eyes I flick his image from my memory into view. Every past word, glance, and touch between us triggers lust, giddiness, and a jubilation I have never felt about anyone before.

Ten days go by and the postcards stop. Maybe it was all a dream, not what I imagined it to be? I push the thought to the very back of my brain and spend no more energy on it. His four postcards are lined up on my desk and every night I turn them over and over in an attempt to read the white spaces for clues. The day he is supposed to return is circled in red in my datebook.

⚡

Greenwich Village celebrates the first sign of hot weather with short shorts, tank tops, and less. Gays, straights, lesbians, cross-dressers, drag kings, and college coeds snake around the streets in a giant pub crawl. Jimmy Day's is smack in the heart of it, extra popular because of buyback bartenders and busboys who push Quaaludes and Bennies on the side for a buck apiece. Jimmy Day hires a bouncer to keep whacked-out Village people from getting in and drunks who have not paid their tabs from getting out.

My brutal late night shift is about over but customers are still three deep at the bar. I pinch through the overflow crowd packed in around my tables to deliver baskets of onion rings and pitchers of Guinness.

At 3:30 a.m., Mel rings the last call bell and everybody groans, then presses closer to the bar to get their last drink orders in. People are desperate, trying to flag me down, waving beer mugs and twenties in the air.

A middle-aged guy in a raincoat slips by Bruno, the bouncer, and tries to make his way to the bar. He throws his arms around a guy in a blue T-shirt who is blocking his way. The blue T-shirt guy turns around and punches Mr. Raincoat in the gut. There is a short scuffle and a woman screams. Mr. Raincoat falls to the floor, while the blue T-shirt guy slips out the door. More people start screaming and someone yells, "He's bleeding!"

With his coat splayed open, blood oozes out of Mr. Raincoat, making a deep red semicircle on the left side of his chest. Bruno grabs a clean tablecloth and presses it against Mr. Raincoat's rib cage.

— Mel! Oh, for Christ's sake. Call the police. Adrienne pushes into the crowd and disappears.

— Bar's closed! Everybody out! Mel cries.

As I slam down checks and pluck money off tables, Mel signals the okay for Adrienne to crack open the back door and the place is empty in ten minutes, except for Mr. Raincoat, who is still on the floor mumbling, "He stabbed me, that motherfucker stabbed me."

— Hey! Close the back door and get over here, Mel calls to me from up front.

— What do you want?

— Your boyfriend's here. The actor.

Mel flips his head toward the front windows.

— He *is* your boyfriend, isn't he?

I glance up and there is Bill, out on the sidewalk, his hand shielding his eyes.

— It's okay, Bruno. You can let him in.

Bruno cracks the front door open and Bill inches through,

sidestepping around Mr. Raincoat to scoop me up in his arms. We remain pressed together for what seems like five minutes.

I feel Mel staring holes through us.

— Can I get a glass of white wine, I shout.

— Bar's closed, Mel barks.

I give Mel a don't-even-think-about-being-an-asshole-tonight look.

— For you, I'll make an exception, he singsongs back.

I pull Bill into the shadows and out of the way. We stand nose to nose, our foreheads touch.

— I brought you something.

Not thinking I hear him correctly, I pull away and point my gaze toward Mr. Raincoat, silent on the floor. A blob of tissue paper rustles between us. Bill has reached into his briefcase and holds out something for me to take. The front door slams open and two cops step inside. An ambulance pulls up. A flurry of rushed movements and Mr. Raincoat is gone. The porter, Pedro, pulls a mop across the floor.

I sense something brush against my stomach, realize Bill still holds the red tissue out to me. Gently, I take it and reach inside to uncover a carved pewter jewelry box lined with green velvet.

— An artist near my father's house made it.

— It's beautiful.

— Turn it over.

I flip the box over. Two words, *Amo te,* are engraved there.

— *Amo te?*

— It means *I love you.*

In the center of my body, just behind my sternum, my heart vibrates.

— I love you.

Bill does not interpret the writing on the bottom of the box now. He looks at me and hums the words. The ends of his lips turn up into a curl. His eyes are wet and transplendent.

Outside, the ambulance lights begin to flash and the siren moans. The sound increases in volume until it is a loud wail calling across

West 4th Street. As the vehicle speeds away the sound fades, floats over Sheridan Square, the Christopher Street Pier, and out across the Hudson River.

Here it comes. Delivered direct.

My body feels as though it will explode; my blood presses against every corner of my skin. I look straight into Bill's Cambridge-blue eyes, hold my breath, and feel my heart split open to drain all the tenderness within through the pores in my fingertips and into the warmth of his huge hand that I hold tightly in mine.

— I love you too.

Then I almost laugh, almost tumble over, almost shoot through the ceiling and into the night sky.

⚡

I am plucked off the face of the earth. Time stops. There is only this moment and all the moments before this moment and all the moments after this moment. What divides them is the single second when, cradled by the universe, I grasp for the adventure I believe I was born to. I will walk a new path, be the explorer of uncharted territory, the discoverer of one true love. With this knowledge firmly in hand I return to solid ground a pioneer.

It had been a long time coming. We had known each other for almost a year. We were friends before we both fell in love. I held him at bay until the timing was right. When it was right we collided, each of us absorbed the other in a mutual adoration. We were two exceptional people who need not waste time on a courtship. This is what human beings do. We cut to the chase, pledge ourselves to each other from the very start. You read about this happening. Well, it happened. To me. He says he has never felt this way before, and I fling myself down to snort up those words like they are last traces of blow I will ever see in my life before he can take them back.

What would have happened to me if I had not? Gripping the before-this-moment and the after-this-moment like a tear in a well-worn garment, I stitch it together to hide the gaping hole I used to think of as my destiny, the only thing left a rough seam. I want a glimpse of what might have been.

When I look back all I can see are warning lights in a hot summer. In 1977 I fell in love. I took the bait, swallowed the hook, gobbled up the line, and would have reeled myself in if you let me. Did I stop to think about how fast it was happening? No. Did I feel even a little bit suspicious of how intense it was from the very start? No. I could have admitted to myself there was something not quite right about the speed and the force of it all. I could have done that. Or I could have been swept off my feet.

⚡

I am walking along Fifth Avenue in my bell-bottom jeans and vintage forest-green jacket I bought for two bucks at Goodwill. The sunlight slants harshly, making shadows across the asphalt. A sky mottled with angel hair clouds is overhead. I have my Naugahyde purse slung over my shoulder and my shiny aviator sunglasses over my eyes. It is three o'clock in the afternoon and I have just gotten up.

I strut across gritty 14th Street, where head shops with bongs and lava lamps in the windows line the corners. I travel past the old row houses in Washington Mews where I imagine bearded NYU professors live, stride by the swanky 1 Fifth Avenue apartment building, cross Washington Square North to step under and through the Washington Square Arch. As I cut a wide path through the park, dealers come out from behind trees and bushes, whispering. Smoke? Loose joint?

The guy who wheels his piano to the park every day is banging out "On Broadway" and singing with gusto. A few people gather around and join in. To the south, on the black asphalt mounds, three aging hippies play bongos and smoke pot. An old lady has gotten her cart stuck in the doorway of the public toilet. She curses loudly. As I head west, a trumpet bleats out notes that float from someone's open window nearby.

I feel in perfect sync with New York City. The clouds move one way above me and the earth moves the other way below me and I am at the center of it all. Even though the air is crisp, the sidewalk emanates a heat I absorb and store away for another day. Suddenly overwhelmed with a rush of optimism, I open my mouth and laugh out loud. I am twenty-three years old. On West 4th Street, at the big front windows of Jimmy Day's Bar and Restaurant, I stop to catch my own sparkling reflection in the glass.

4

1997, NEW YORK CITY

A RAINY FRIDAY AFTERNOON. I STARE out the window of my apartment on the thirty-second floor in Battery Park City. Tiny ferryboats full of midday commuters crisscross the Hudson River to and from New Jersey to dump New York–bound passengers next to the World Financial Center in the wind and rain. Flimsy umbrellas pop awkwardly as women and men in business suits race towards the shelter of their office buildings. I look to my right and 1 World Trade Center looms into the sky, the top obscured by mist and fog. My ear is pressed to the phone. I have no idea who is on the other end of the line.

— Who did you say you were?

— It's Gertrude Stein, Guerrilla Girl, on the line. You've been recommended as someone who is interested in becoming a Guerrilla Girl. I'm calling to let you know there will be a secret meeting in a loft downtown next week.

— What? I mean, yes, I would be honored. Where is the . . .

— I'll give you the address and the password.

— Fine. Sure.

— You cannot share this information with anyone, got it?

— GOT IT!

I remind myself to not speak so loudly as I dive across the couch for a pen and a piece of paper.

— You will have to swear on a stack of bananas that you will never reveal the real identity of any other Guerrilla Girl when you arrive. Hello?

— I'll swear. For sure.

Gertrude gives me the address and password. I scribble them on the first piece of paper I can grab.

— That's not all.

— What? What else?

— See you there.

Click.

I listen to the silence, look at the address and password scrawled on a Century 21 department store receipt, imagine myself memorizing the info and swallowing the paper with a glass of Merlot. I settle for just a glass of Merlot and burn the paper in the sink, watch the flames die until a black mark on the stainless steel is all that remains.

The night I go underground the air is crisp, the wind calm. I take the elevator to the lobby and walk out the revolving doors of my apartment building in Gateway Plaza. I pass the security gate guarding Gateway's oval drive, cross South End Avenue, swoosh through the revolving doors of 1 World Financial Center, board the up escalator to the south bridge, march above and over West Street to Liberty Street, and enter the Marriott Hotel. I snake around the staircase in the lobby of the Marriott, skate through the doors of the shopping concourse underneath the World Trade Center to take all the shortcuts my body has memorized in the three years I have lived downtown. The storefronts I know so well tick by: Banana Republic on my right, Gap on my left. I make a turn and head straight for Watch World, then another turn at Godiva Chocolatier, past Manchenko Te Sushi, Nine West, and finally land at Borders, Mrs. Fields, Pretzel Time, and the entrance to the E train. I slip my token in the slot, hit my hip against the turnstile, and jump on the train about to depart north toward SoHo.

I arrive twenty minutes early, so I find the address and then wander the streets until it is five minutes past the meeting time. As I approach the building I mouth the password several times, trying my best to sound ballsy. I find the apartment number and buzz the buzzer. "Hot Flash," I say into the intercom, not quite delivering it as practiced and feeling a little silly. The buzzer buzzes, I step into the elevator and ride up. After a minute the door opens directly onto a narrow hallway where a woman wearing a big black rubber gorilla mask stands, a glass of wine balanced between her fingers.

WOMAN: HI! WELCOME! I'M ALICE NEEL![6] CAN YOU HEAR ME?

ME: Hi. Did you say your name was Alice?

ALICE: WHAT? IT'S HARD TO HEAR WHEN YOU'RE WEARING A MASK.

ME: Oh.

ALICE: ANYWAY, LIKE I SAID, I'M ALICE NEEL AND I DIED IN 1984.

ME: I'm ready to swear on the stack of bananas.

ALICE: OH, GO ON! YOU'RE A RIOT! GERTRUDE, ANOTHER ONE WHO WANTS TO SWEAR ON A BANANA! GET IN THERE!

Alice puts her hand on my shoulder and with an enthusiastic shove pushes me toward the middle of her loft where twenty or so unmasked women stand around with wineglasses, beer bottles, and plates of Chinese takeout in hand.

It did not sink in until minutes later that Alice Neel was not really Alice Neel. Only later did I learn that Alice Neel was a pioneering American artist who painted portraits of left-wing politicians, civil rights activists, and second-wave feminists from the '30s until her

---

6 Alice Neel (1900–1984), Expressionist portraitist of both famous and ordinary people of the 20th century.

death in the early '80s. Alice Neel was the Guerrilla Girl name chosen by the hostess of the meeting.

My mentor, Lyubov Popova, is not present, having officially retired after twelve years of service. However, we do speak days before the meeting and she guarantees at the very least there will be decent food, plenty of wine, and some very interesting women to meet.

I grab a beer and introduce myself around. I have no idea if people are giving me their real names or their Guerrilla Girl names. Finally, I bump into Gertrude Stein, who has a big, bright smile, shining eyes, and tremendous laugh. "Welcome to the Guerrilla Girls," Gertrude barks. She hands me a piece of paper. "Welcome to the Guerrilla Girls" is written at the top and a summary of the history of the group follows. They began in 1985 as a response to an exhibit of contemporary art at MOMA of 169 artists, of whom only thirteen were women, even fewer were artists of color, and zero were women artists of color. They remain committed to critiquing the art world and beyond. Each of them goes by the name of a dead woman artist.

Gertrude motions for me to sit next to her as everyone begins to settle into a circle of mismatched chairs in the middle of the loft. The official meeting is about to begin.

Alice Neel is joined by another Guerrilla Girl who calls herself Alma Thomas.[7] Alma also sports a rubber gorilla mask, frozen in an openmouthed, angry expression. Both masks are covered in matted black polyester fur. Visually they are frightening, and when Alice and Alma speak their voices are distorted and faint. Alma and Alice describe what it is like to wear a rubber gorilla mask for hours at a time (a feeling akin to being simultaneously gagged and menopausal). To me, they sound as if they are inside a steam shower.

The theatre person in me knows that wearing a mask is liberating and donning a disguise can foster a unique sense of autonomy. Who would not want to free themselves of their own limitations and fears

---

7 Alma Thomas (1891–1978), abstract expressionist painter and art educator.

by being somebody else for a while? But the masks completely block Alma's and Alice's facial expressions. The menacing look on the gorilla disguises contrasts their funny statements and animated bodies and thus the stiff rubber masks are actually an obstruction between us. I have to lean in to understand what they are saying. I wonder if anyone has ever thought about how distancing the Guerrilla Girl signature look actually is.

I would tackle the mask problem at a later date when, together with Lorraine Hansberry, I write a play entitled *The History of Women in Theatre* for the A.S.K. Common Ground Festival. The festival organizers put Lorraine and me in touch with a designer who cuts our gorilla masks in half and substitutes wigs for the matted fake fur. These new gorilla looks expose half our faces and are ultimately better for performances because they eliminate part of the obstacle the rubber gorilla masks present.

Back at my first Guerrilla Girl meeting, Alice and Alma explain how and why they chose their particular pseudonyms.

— It is a very personal assignment, Alma remarks, and should be approached with seriousness. You will use this name in public and in many ways be the standard-bearer for that particular dead woman artist during your career as a Guerrilla Girl.

— The name you pick will be your Guerrilla Girl persona for all public appearances like lectures and interviews, Alice adds.

The names taken by the Guerrilla Girls also serve a pedagogical function. They provide the opportunity to reverse the biases of history by putting the lives and works of neglected women artists into the public eye. I learn that some Girls refused to take names (they take numbers instead), and some take one name only to come to realize it does not work for them and wind up choosing another. The names and masks are important because they give the Guerrilla Girls a unique position: From a masked, pseudonymous point of view they can freely critique the art world, a world they are all very much a part of. None of the members anticipated the buzz the masks and the pseudonyms would create. Almost from day one there has been a lot of speculation about who the Guerrilla Girls really are.

I am about to join a secret society. I feel hip and cool and full of inspiration.

After Alice and Alma's presentation everyone goes around and introduces themselves and their herstory with the Girls. All possess an enviable confidence that borders on narcissism. These women artists cut each other off with insider art world jokes that result in minutes of raucous laughter and insightful screams. The energy between them crackles. They are in cahoots about something mysterious and addictive. It is suddenly a bit intimidating and I find myself thinking hard about what I am going to say when, thankfully, one of the other new recruits is up to introduce herself first.

How a Meeting Can Turn into a Panel Discussion
in the Blink of an Eye
A very short play

NEW RECRUIT

Hello. I'm a writer. I write about women and women's work. I am so honored to be joining this diverse group.

ALMA THOMAS

(pulling off gorilla mask) You did notice that there are very few women of color in the room, did you not?

(The AIR is suddenly sucked out of the room. ICE in everyone's Chablis begins to melt. Characters improvise an argument on racism and white privilege for ten minutes.)

What just happened? In a few seconds the celebratory introductory meeting has turned into a wordy debate. Even though the group acts politely, there is an obvious tension between some Guerrilla Girls. Us six or seven newbies sit silently and watch as the Girls go from guffawing girlfriends to suspicious sisters. Even so, this "panel discussion" carries the weight of importance and is a conversation I suspect the Guerrilla Girls have had before.

Second divisive tactic noted: Guerrilla Girl meetings can flip on a dime. Also noted was this: just because a bunch of women gather in the name of feminism does not mean there will not be division akin to the patriarchal world we are trying to transform.

FACT: IN THE JUNGLE REAL GORILLAS HAVE LIMITED FEMALE RELATIONSHIPS AND MULTIPLE AGGRESSIVE ENCOUNTERS.

As a member of the Guerrilla Girls, I participated in many discussions on sexism and race. Gender was not the only factor in discrimination against artists. Statistically, women artists of color and artists of color in general are underrepresented in the arts much more so than white women. During my time as a Girl we made an effort to be as inclusive a group as we could be, to include many voices, to look at all sides of discrimination. When I joined in 1997, however, the number of active members who were women of color fluctuated. Still, discussions about patriarchy as it related to race, to class, to age, to sexual identity, and to gender cropped up whenever we talked about future projects. A lot of issues were discussed and tabled and discussed again. The group functioned on consensus and majority rule most of the time. I say most of the time because forward-moving energy was not always easy to maintain. Sometimes our numbers in meetings were low. Even so, terminology was always on the agenda. Should we call for better representation for women, or for women and women of color, or for white women and women of color, or for artists of color and women? We changed the wording on posters as we evolved. And while we shied away from talking in public about our personal lives as artists, we learned a lot from each other by sharing, in private, stories and struggles during meetings. As we strove for parity in our own ranks it was often difficult and we did not always succeed. When as a group we came up with something we had equally contributed to and were all proud of, it felt like a major shift in the right direction.

— Let's move on. Do we have any questions from the newcomers?

I raise my hand.

— How do things get accomplished? What are the rules? Who is in charge? How do you divide up the work?

— We gather in small groups to work on each poster. A majority vote from everyone present puts a poster into production. No one is in charge. We are all equal. We meet every twenty-eight days.

At this first meeting it is clear to me that several people think they are in charge or want to be in charge or hope that those who believe they are in charge are actually not in charge. It is also obvious no one is in charge and that there is no set structure of the Girls, with the exception that certain Girls have jobs like balancing the checkbook or fielding queries about appearances and poster sales. Those Girls have whatever power their job dictates, and yet I understand from this first meeting that the Guerrilla Girls are more or less an unstructured group with a free-for-all feel. I am both baffled and enchanted by this unorganized mess of feminists.

My mind goes over all of the ways I think discrimination in theatre might be addressed by the Girls. This meeting is simply a meet-and-greet; no activist work will be done. As the meeting part of the evening begins to lose steam, Alice encourages all us newbies to think about the name of a dead woman artist we would like to take as new Guerrilla Girls.

As the Girls jump up to refill their drinks and grab some more egg rolls, I receive pats on the back from women who warmly welcome me and urge me to choose a name and buy a mask (which the Girls will reimburse me for). I already know who I want to be: Aphra Behn,[8] seventeenth-century playwright and poet who herself had used a few different pseudonyms. She wrote bawdy plays with feminist themes. She has the same number of syllables as my real name. I take Aphra Behn as my Guerrilla Girl pseudonym and for almost two decades get as comfortable answering to it as to the name I was born with.

A few weeks later I visit Abracadabra on West 21st Street and purchase the friendliest-looking gorilla mask I can find for fifty bucks. With the goal to make my gorilla look approachable, I highlight Aphra Behn's frozen face by painting her lips red and sticking pink bows in her fake fur. At least she has one gentle feature. Her teeth are rotten. Soon afterward, and even though I did not do a smidgen of work on it, the Girls invite all new and old members to a book signing at the Lincoln Center Barnes & Noble to celebrate the publication of *The Guerrilla Girls' Bedside Companion to the History of Western Art*. It will be my first public appearance as the gorilla-mask-wearing Guerrilla Girl Aphra Behn.

I am walking along Columbus Avenue in my boot-cut jeans and black leather jacket. In the alcove of a building on the corner of 67th Street, a half dozen women press together, pull gorilla masks out of their handbags, gather their hair into ponytails, and slip the masks over their heads. I squeeze in beside one of them and pull my own gorilla mask on. Immediately I feel my quick exhalations steam up the inside

---

8 Aphra Behn (1640–1689), prolific dramatist of the English Restoration.

of the mask. Moisture gathers around the nose holes and the mask slips below my eyes. I cannot see a thing.

The pack of Guerrilla Girls is on the move now and I scurry behind, pulling the fake fur on top of my head up so I can keep the eyeholes of my mask aligned and spy which direction the Girls are headed. As I fall in line with the bunch of them, I turn to a Guerrilla Girl to say something when I realize I have no idea who anyone is anymore. I lean into the Girl on my right and shout, "Who are you?" She either does not hear me or is more focused on not bumping into buildings. I keep pace with the group as together we strut down the street, a band of masked women, some of us in heels and fishnet stockings, others sporting combat boots and leopardskin gloves. I wear a colorful scarf twisted around a black turtleneck sweater.

Once we are through the revolving door of Barnes & Noble, four or five photographers step forward. *Click, click, click.* They lean backwards to create a path between themselves so we can make our way to the elevator. *Click, click, click.*

A Barnes & Noble staff member holds open the elevator doors. An aggressive photographer pushes his way onto the elevator with us. *Click, click, click.*

We rise to the third floor. The doors open onto a room deep with people. Their heads turn simultaneously as one by one we pop out of the elevator. I latch eyes with a woman who looks at me adoringly. I think she might be drooling.

We are led to a long table and each take a seat behind it. Two Guerrilla Girls stand at an adjacent podium and take turns reading from the book. When the audience laughs I follow the other Guerrilla Girls' lead and grunt, pounding my fists on the table. *Click, click, click.*

Someone passes over a bunch of bananas. We raise the bananas high in the air and screech when the reading is over. A line begins to form in front of us. Fans squeeze in to present to us their purchased copies of *The Guerrilla Girls' Bedside Companion to the History of Western Art*. The first Girl at the table opens the book to the first page and signs her name. She passes the book to the next Girl, and on and on until it gets to me. I pick up a pen.

I sign the book, "Aphra Behn #160,"[9] in sloppy round letters. *Click, click, click.* I feel in perfect sync with New York City. No one knows who I really am.

---

9 Aphra Behn was employed as a spy by Charles II and was known as Agent 160.

5

1960S AND '70S, LONG ISLAND, NEW YORK

I GROW UP WITH MUSIC. IT comes from the car radio or from the record player in the living room or from my mother's mouth. She is always singing, and the words to her songs often stop me from what I am doing to ponder: What is it like to land in a pot of jam? How do you put on some speed? Where exactly is the beguine? Among the albums sloppily stacked next to the stereo, my favorite is a five-LP box set from Time-Life of great classical music.

I grow up with words. Thumbed-through *Life* magazines and Sears catalogs make way every month for the arrival of another volume of *The Golden Book Encyclopedia,* delivered via U.S. mail, until all sixteen of them line a corner of my room.

I grow up with props. Discarded buoys dragged home from the marina across the street or metal doodads from the dump down the block are stashed behind the garage for future use. Inside the hall closet a barrel full of canteens, green utility belts, and World War II army helmets awaits, passed down to me when my older brothers tire of them.

Sounds, language, objects make up my uberous childhood. I am a hungry girl in search of what feeds me. What feeds me is making stuff up.

In my daily hunt around the house for ideas, I come across a spiral notebook, a baseball bat, a half-filled ten-cent coloring book, a heavy roll of white butcher paper, an old and very out-of-tune piano, and the guitar my parents purchased for me with Green Stamps.

My thoughts grow large. They make me laugh out loud. The things I think jump and multiply and fly like pellets from a shotgun from somewhere deep within.

Suddenly, a clap of thunder goes off inside my brain and like a puzzle I feel all the pieces of my unadulterated female self snap together.

I grab a pencil, the small spiral notebook, and run out the side door. The screen hisses slowly to a close behind me. A small vibrating ping just behind my sternum keeps a steady beat. The tiny tap pressing against the middle of my chest from the inside out feels most pleasant and full of energy.

I bound up two short steps and into the side yard. It is spring warm. The air holds traces of gasoline and lilacs. Climbing up the clay bank to the tree with the root shaped like a stool, I stop, crouch, open the notebook, and poise the pencil over the page.

Positioned high above my universe, I survey what is before me. Looking from left to right I see the roof of my house and garage, the fence, the sidewalk, and beyond that the white brick building across the street that says GLEN COVE MARINA above the windows in black block lettering. The tippy tops of a few masts from the sailboats moored in the harbor directly behind the building prick the sky, their halyards sing a fairy song of tiny metal drums, *ting, ting, ting*ing oh so softly in the distance. Beyond the harbor an outline of evergreen treetops pushes against a blue, cloudless backdrop. To the right, the tungsten factory's beige chimney exhales weak balls of black smoke.

The tings of the halyards and the pings in my chest sync up. I blur the vision in my eyes and focus as far as I can see beyond the smoke and trees. Then, like a movie camera, I pull the focus toward me and concentrate on the halyards; the white brick and black lettering; my mom's pink rosebushes slumped across the wood fence; the roof of my garage; and finally the bark of the tree trunk next to me. I see everything, even the air, which looks like tiny black-and-white polka dots floating lazily in front of my face.

I open the notebook. The letters snap from my core through the lead in the pencil and exit as dark slashes on the page. The words surge forward in waves, crashing down as slanted consonants and spiral vowels before receding once again. I turn myself inside out, take by force my leaking heart, transform it into a physical object: charcoal-grey words on blue-lined white paper. I disappear from the world only to reemerge a captive of the joyful essence of whom I was just minutes ago, transformed into something I can hold in my hand.

The ice-cream truck bell chimes somewhere up the street. From the sound I guess it has stopped at Putnam Avenue. I shut the notebook and climb farther up the bank, walking south on the path I have forged that sews together all the backyards of the houses on my block. Stepping over newly sprouted vines, maple saplings, and young sumac trees, I become the place where I am completely alone. I linger for a moment to relish the thoughts—no one can see me, no one knows where I am.

I duck under a low branch, hold on to an exposed root covered in green moss, and slide past the Malloys' old garage until I come to Mr. Furst's long gravel driveway. His car is not there and his house sits silent.

I open the notebook and read my words. I change a few sentences and close my eyes in satisfaction. "*. . . and never another word written.*"

Overhead a puff of a cloud moves across the sky. A car swooshes past on the road below. I race down the sloping incline of the driveway to my block, make a right, and walk past the front of the Malloys' house. My right hand brushes against the overgrown hedgerow invading the slats of Mr. Malloy's crumbling front porch until I turn right into my driveway. A short jog up the blacktop takes me back to the very same side door I exited out of just twenty minutes ago. I race past the kitchen and up the steps to the second floor, slide on the waxed linoleum to the end of the hall, and throw open the door to my room.

The notebook, hot in my hand, is shoved into the bottom drawer of my painted pressboard desk alongside all the others I have stashed away there. I slam the drawer shut and flop backwards onto my bed. I see the pane of glass in the window and then through the glass to the upper branches of the maple tree in my front yard.

The ice-cream truck creeps down the street. I hear my sister's voice call for me up the stairs. Inside the freezer in the rear of the truck the ice-cream bars on wooden sticks are lined up in rows inside their paper wrappings. I think about the orange of the Creamsicle, the copper of the toasted almond. I recall how shiny the vanilla is.

Downstairs the side door clicks open and eases shut. I get up off the bed and see my sister's straight blonde hair fly across the lawn. The ice-cream truck has stopped right in front of my house and waits for me.

$$\lightning$$

Other days I occupy a different world, a world of silence and severity. A universe of boredom. The world of blah. The sharp edges of my unique self are shaved down to nubs, my impulses washed out. I sit where I am told and stand when I am told. Shushed and pushed into and out of lines, my small body must keep very still so it might be schooled.

The first thing I learn is I must learn. If I do not absorb every piece of knowledge imparted to me by the benevolent Sisters of Mercy, I will wind up a failure. I concentrate as best I can to the first lessons: reading, writing, and repenting.

— Pay attention to your soul, Sister Remigis says. Your soul is like a blank square of white poster board. When you were born, your white poster board soul had an ugly black smear on it. The smear was Original Sin. Everyone is born with Original Sin because, instead of choosing God, Eve chose herself when she ate the apple off the Tree of

Knowledge. Eve was a selfish woman and now everyone has to suffer because of her.

Maybe Eve was just a hungry girl like me, I think to myself.

Luckily, I learn that my own Original Sin has been permanently erased when I was baptized Roman Catholic. Unfortunately, there are two other types of sin out there that can still mess up my white poster board soul: mortal sin and venial sin. Venial sins are tiny sins like chewing gum in class or wearing your bangs too long. When you commit a venial sin a tiny black dot shows up on your white poster board soul. Mortal sins are gigantic sins like murder and not going to church on Sunday. If you commit a mortal sin your white poster board soul is almost completely covered with a big black splotch. Only venial sins can be wiped away by going to confession and saying out loud you are very sorry. Mortal sins stay on your soul forever and you go to hell when you die, but you should still say you are sorry on the off chance you are selected for Purgatory, a kind of vacation spot for dead people to catch up on repenting.

I am suspicious about what I am taught about my soul. It makes more sense to me that my soul is what causes the stretch and pull I feel inside when I make something up. This soul is not white or marred or poster board-like at all. When I close my eyes I see my soul as translucent and silver, speckled with veins of cobalt blue. In the world of blah I fear having this vision might be a sin itself.

⚡

After school I take dance lessons at Miss M.'s School of Dancing. Miss M. loves my sister, Dynie, because she has a perfect foot with a high arch. I have a stiff foot attached to a rigid leg and an inflexible torso. But I have rhythm. Miss M. shows me a step and I repeat it perfectly. Miss M. rolls her eyes and I know she thinks having perfect rhythm is nothing if you do not have a perfect foot. She puts me in the last row in every routine. She keeps me from performing with the advanced tappers. At home I put the *1812 Overture* from the five-LP box set of great classical music from Time-Life on the stereo and choreograph my own routine to the music, interpreting the glorious sounds with quivering limbs. When I perform, a light emanates from the unquenchable bloom of my soul, and I feel as if I can harness enough power to save the world. I believe people with both perfect feet and imperfect feet can dance, even if Miss M. does not admit it.

My mom drives my sister and me to Miss M.'s every week until we graduate high school. All those years Miss M. continues to overlook my ability even as it gleams before her very eyes.

⚡

The road I live on is divided. Irish, Polish, German, Greek, Hungarian, and Italian immigrant households are to the west, while African-American households are to the east. My house sits smack in the middle of the two. Being at the very center, I identify with everyone around me.

As I grow up I become subtly aware of an invisible fence zigzagging through the neighborhood, separating the families in the houses on my block. I begin to crisscross back and forth from one side of the street to the other when I ride my bike to the beach at the end of the road. Slowly I memorize the places I do not belong, am not allowed, must not occupy.

My older brothers, Kenny and Ray, come home from school with pencil cases missing, torn jackets, milk money gone. My parents do not talk in the yard with the neighbors as often as they used to. In school, I am made fun of for where I live. When I come home crying, Mom leaves a note under my pillow with these words: "It's not where you live but how you live."

How I live feels smaller. Instead of sensing I am right in the middle of things, I am sharply aware of how separated I am from parts of it now. It feels as if my entire family suddenly woke up and discovered that our neighborhood had changed.

The connection I have to myself and my neighborhood is harnessed. There is something different about it I begin to be ashamed of. I feel myself splitting in two.

⚡

I am saved by Girl Scout camp, a seamless universe ruled by girls in East Hampton, Long Island, just eighty-three miles from where I live but a universe away. The first year I go with a classmate from fifth grade. The next year with my sister. I spend the next ten summers of my life in an all-female world without borders or separations, aka Camp Blue Bay.

My gang forms the very first year. Our nicknames—Toni, Bruno, Val, Corky, Kaz, Flash—reinforce our new identities as a spontaneous, girl-spirit artistic collective. We are governed by cooperation, solidarity, teamwork, and ritual. Ideas sputter and spit between us like downed power lines.

Camp serves as an incubator for our group work. We invent a final campfire, featuring a flaming ball of gasoline-soaked Kotex pads suspended from a wire at the top of a bluff and rigged to land in a log-cabin-laid fire pit fifty yards below. When it hits the target it explodes into an inferno as big as a playhouse.

Our gang is pure female ingenuity. What we do together lingers, is unforgettable, is possible because something about the open air and the dense woods and the expansive ocean reminds us there are no limits to what we set our minds to. We understand we have the physical and mental strength to accomplish any goal.

For those few weeks each summer I feel I am the most myself. After days of laughing so hard I cry, from sunup to lights-out, my inner comedienne rises and I comprehend for the first time that humor is and will always be my guiding star. I am a funny girl, and as long as I hang on to my wit I will never completely lose my way.

⚡

I reach high school just as the world around me rises up. The television and newspapers boast a churning of civil unrest and protest. Vietnam, civil rights, women's rights, black power, flower power, Woodstock, Kent State are headlines. I am not old enough to join the massive movement of the youth, who carry the country on their backs and will not give in until their demands to stop the war, stop sexism, stop racism are met. I watch it unfold on TV in the safety of my living room, slip a black armband around the sleeve of my Nehru jacket, a POW bracelet engraved with the name of Captain Ronald Mastin and the date 1-16-67 on my wrist, and play the live Woodstock album over and over with the volume knob cranked as loud as it can go.

I am now both a teenager and female and thus occupy a special place in the era of low self-esteem. The fearless female self I am in the summer does not translate into adolescence, and I experience an even greater split in selves. Overemotional, I burst into tears at least five times a day for no apparent reason. I am completely self-obsessed and I resent having to think about anything except how shitty my fall, winter, and spring life is compared to the summer when I can don my secret, strong, and confident identity. The person I am in high school is desperate to be in with the in crowd yet incapable of participating at all in humankind. Feeling like I exist deep inside a hole, I float in the background, view life from behind a wall, daydream my escape from what I am on paper: a regular student with a B-plus average and mediocre SAT scores, about to be sucked forever into the swirling vortex of the world of blah and the era of low self-esteem. But my parents' never-ending praise encourages me to grab for one last chance called college.

$$\displaystyle \Large \frac{\;}{\;}\,\bigstar$$

In an effort to elevate myself to the high standards of art I believe I am capable of, I apply to NYU for dance, which requires an audition.

Now I turn my brooding over to the conception of a three-minute dance piece and select the overture of *Jesus Christ Superstar* as my music. I pour all of my anxiety and anger into the piece, a free-form flinging of arms, legs, and torso executed with precise rhythm. There is nothing religious about my interpretation, only the fact that when I perform it I feel like Jesus, or how I think Jesus must have felt, which makes me consider why the Catholic Church never offered me any female role models besides the Virgin Mary, a woman so pure I could never relate to her. Then I think about how I really never had any female role models, period. The majority of the artists I am exposed to are male. No matter; I will change all that. I use the time when everyone is out of the house to practice my routine in the living room. Not showing it to anyone gives me the security of self-assessment. If it feels good it is good.

On the day of the audition my older brother Ray accompanies me on the Long Island Rail Road into Manhattan, where I flip-flop between feeling invincible and brainless, settling on a quiet queasiness that increases the closer we get to NYU.

The audition, on Second Avenue between 6th and 7th, in a building boasting a Tisch School of the Arts banner, cannot be over soon enough, and, thankfully, my brother agrees to drop me off and pick me up in an hour's time. I join a bunch of other prospective students in an old dressing room lined with lockers, and while the others pull their hair into tight buns, slip into dance skirts and ballet slippers, I take off my coat and shoes and slide leg warmers over my ankles. I have chosen to wear a claret-colored leotard and bell-bottoms, which, to avoid the embarrassment of having to change in front of strangers, I already have on.

The only thing I remember about the audition is the end. While I pant wildly and remove my LP from the portable stereo, a faculty juror on the audition panel asks me why I chose to wear bell-bottoms instead of dance clothes.

— I am wearing what I think is the most appropriate outfit for my work, is my reply.

Why should all dancers look the same? I think to myself as I run from the room, bursting with the joy of having it all over with. There is nothing more I can do now. I leave it in the hands of the universe.

A few weeks later I receive a letter from NYU informing me I have not been accepted into the dance department but I have been offered admittance into the dance education department. I am extremely disappointed and use the rejection to confirm my self-assessed mediocrity.

In retrospect, I realize an acceptance into the dance education department is something I might have been convinced to look at in another way. They must have seen something in me and my dance. I could have been proud of the alternative acceptance, but I was too engrossed in the era of low self-esteem and imagined it was possible they gave everyone who auditioned the very same choice. I am still no one special.

⚡

My ever-patient parents, who do not have college degrees, have saved up enough money to pay for my entire college tuition provided I get admitted into a state school or a community college (approximately $1,000 per semester in 1972). But in 1972 there is a swell of baby boomer applicants and college is not easy to get into.

I do not want to be a dance teacher and NYU is too expensive anyway. There is just one state university in New York that has a dance department at the time, and that is SUNY Brockport. They require no audition. But I do not get in there either. I hastily apply to two local community colleges and am rejected by them as well.

With the days draining away toward spring and high school graduation, my father suggests I apply to a private, local school and take out student loans. I apply to Hofstra and get in. My future will not include living in a dorm, which I envision as the same as having my own artist's studio and even better than Camp Blue Bay. No, I will live at home and commute to Hofstra in the fall.

Thank you, universe, for the perfect scenario for me, an overemotional teenager who believes she is a complete failure, to totally commit to. *I am so worthless I cannot even get into college!*

And then, just as I don the pathetic, stiff pout and slumping posture I will adopt as a morose and reluctant incoming freshman, only days after I send in my deposit to Hofstra, SUNY Brockport sends me a letter explaining that a spot has opened up and offers me a place in the class of 1976.

6

1972–76, BROCKPORT, NEW YORK

AUGUST 1972: IN THE REGISTRATION LINE at Brockport's freshman orientation, I repeat to myself the words "theatre, dance, theatre, dance." The line leads to a table of employees who record each incoming freshman's major and register them for the appropriate classes. Would I, the inflexible, stiff-footed dancer, ever find a place in the dance world? Or should I branch out and set my sights on an art form where my dance training might come in handy? Suddenly I am up.

— Major? Major?

— I'm thinking!

— You don't have to declare a major today. You can do it next semester.

— No! I have to do it now.

— Well then, what'll it be?

— Theatre!

With a dithyrambic lilt to my voice, I declare theatre as my major. Theatre! I will be an actress! Theatre will be the route whereby I will combine all of my creative skills—dancing, drawing, writing, weeping.

P.S. I have never acted in my life.

⚡

SUNY Brockport has almost two hundred theatre majors and in the
'70s is led by Professor Joe Talarowski, a kind and generous man whose
office door is always open. Housed in a wing of the Tower Fine Arts
Building, the department boasts four slick main-stage productions a
year. With a full costume shop, construction shop, black-box theatre,
several rehearsal studios, a green room, and a gorgeous four-hundred-
seat theatre with fly and wing space, the department is one of SUNY's
best. On the faculty is the acclaimed experimental theatre historian E.
T. Kirby.

Theatre majors are required to take two semesters of Production
Arts, which means my first months at college are spent on the stage
building sets, hanging lights, and, once the shows are up, assisting
backstage during performances. I love being on the stage, even if it is
just to paint flats and lurk in the wings. My first show is E. T. Kirby's
cutting-edge black-and-white version of Alfred Jarry's *Ubu Roi*. The
actors wear white oversized masks and costumes against a bare stage
hung with black velvet stage drapes. Kirby attempts to light the entire
production using only blacklights, an effect that has never been tried
before. It is not feasible but is an exciting effort and I am there. A
big musical is staged next, *Fiddler on the Roof*, a collaboration with the
music department's orchestra and the dance department faculty and
students. I am assigned the very important job of helping the student
playing Tevye make his quick changes in the wings.

Free to contrive a unique identity, my freshman year of college
revolves around the invention of a new, adult me. Theatre is a collaboration, a group effort, a team-building experience. These are things I
am already Girl-Scout-good at. I sign up for a class in improvisation.
The professor, Gisela Fritzsching, is jovial and supportive and gives me
an A. I am on my way to being an actress.

↯

Before I begin my second year, an actor from Los Angeles is hired
to head Brockport's acting program. Professor B.'s résumé is littered

with commercials and minor roles on TV shows like *Ripcord* and *Perry Mason*. At six foot two with jet-black (dyed) hair, he is all Hollywood, sporting ascots and turtleneck sweaters under gold-buttoned blazers. The color of his trousers often matches his suede ankle boots. His voice pops from his barrel chest in short blasts.

In the fall of 1973 I enroll in Acting I. Professor B.'s class is held in a drab grey basement studio with no heat. He begins with meandering anecdotes about a television pilot he shot or a movie he worked on, flicking his fingers through his hair and taking off his glasses for extra emphasis. He aims to dazzle us with his vast experience, but the class is unimpressed. We are young kids from across the state whose only experience in TV and film has been to watch it at home during breaks. We do not have televisions in our dorm rooms. Most every night we hang out, smoke pot and glean meaningful insights from listening to the Firesign Theatre or David Bowie on our portable stereos. The TV series Professor B. brags about have long since been canceled. When Professor B. tires of talking he reads aloud from articles in theatre journals about different acting techniques and instructs us to stand up and physically interpret what he reads.

— All right, class, let's wheel it around the room, he commands, swinging his arms and indicating that we should all stand up and begin "wheeling it." The twelve or so of us in class stare at each other for a few minutes and then shuffle to our feet, fashion our hands into fists, and walk in a circle while pumping our arms up and down.

— Faster, comes the directive from Professor B. Move faster!

Our strolls turn to race walks. We steal glances at each other and mimic the person we believe is the best physical interpreter of Professor B.'s instructions.

— Now change direction! Professor B. commands. We twist on our toes, race walk in the opposite direction while we cleverly reverse the circles of our fists.

Once we have "wheeling" mastered, Professor B. reads to us about Grotowski's "Plastiques" and Meyerhold's "Biomechanics." Grotowski and Meyerhold were avant-garde theatre pioneers. The techniques they developed emphasized crafting a character by utilizing physical skills and stylized movements. Both men developed their concepts in response to Stanislavsky's "Method" of acting, rooted in emotional memory.

— All right, class, listen and interpret! Fall to the floor; rise on your right foot, shift your weight from your right foot to your left foot and back to your right; describe an arc with your shoulder; draw an imaginary bow; fire with a shout; spring into a position of refusal . . . and on and on Professor B drones. He reads from an article about a Meyerhold exercise called "shooting the bow." I do the best I can to decipher and execute his orders without cracking up.

After physical warm-ups come vocal exercises.

— Everyone say, Ahhhhhhh! Use your diaphragm!

We stand in a straight line against the wall as Professor B. asks each of us to feel his cementlike rib cage while he blasts us with the power of his own voice. Next come tongue-twisters.

Day after day we wheel it around the room, attempt positions of refusal, and feel Professor B.'s stomach. It is playful but not very educational. I expect I am learning about acting, but since I have no experience I am not sure.

Finally, Professor B. pairs us up and assigns us scenes. My first acting role will be the proud, vivacious, and charming Amanda Wingfield from *The Glass Menagerie,* by Tennessee Williams.

What?! I am much more like Amanda Wingfield's twenty-three-year-old, painfully shy and withdrawn daughter, Laura.

— Mr. Professor B.?

— Call me Ben!

— I have a question about my scene.

— Come to my office at four and we'll talk about it.

That afternoon Professor B. waves me into his office, tells me to take a seat, and locks the door. Before I can ask him about my scene his mouth opens and words of sugary praise flow out. Professor B. thinks I have talent. How does he know this, I wonder as I watch him describe me in a way that makes me blush. Could he have deduced all of this from the way I "wheel it" around the room or "shoot the bow"? Within minutes he rolls his desk chair close to mine and tells me he is going to make me a star.

Yep.

A star.

I am going straight to the top.

Why, of course I am.

$$\text{\Large ⚡}$$

The sexual revolution may have exploded in the 1970s, but it had not yet reached me in upstate New York. No one talked about sexual harassment because hardly anyone talked about sex. My world was stuck in stereotypes. Professors could be curmudgeonly, cool, or creepy. Coeds were easy, prudes, or going steady. Aggressive behavior was expected from men. The relatively new medium—television—fell in line with magazines, movies, and books in promoting men as dominant and women as compliant. Incoming freshmen had little in the way of resources available to them if they were assaulted or harassed. Consent? What was that? If you were a woman all you had to do was make sure you did not wear short skirts or walk home alone late at night and nothing bad would happen to you. Rape myths reigned.

$$\text{\Large ⚡}$$

Professor B.'s belief in my talent tosses aside any doubts I harbor of not being able to play the faded southern belle Amanda Wingfield. I am the future of American theatre and therefore am capable of playing any role. Wearing bell-bottom jeans and platform shoes, I clomp into my first acting assignment affecting a bad southern drawl and an overarching attitude of self-importance, screeching about all of the ways my daughter, Laura, has disappointed me. I stink. Professor B. thinks I am brilliant.

I acquiesce to Professor B.'s promise to guide me to stardom and drop by his office at least once a week to discuss my career. Each time I knock he waves me in and locks the door. The first few minutes are always spent talking about my classwork and assignments and how much he is going to help me. After five minutes his face takes on a strange look and he appears to be short of breath. At that point he quickly lifts me off my seat, gives me a bear hug, unlocks the door, and sends me on my way.

This continues until the day his hug turns into a kiss on the cheek. The next time he gives me a peck on the lips. The peck on the lips grows longer and longer, until the day Professor B. shoves his tongue in my mouth and puts his hands on my breasts. Soon after, he unzips his pants, takes out his penis, and pushes my head down. I freeze. Professor B. is fifty-four years old. I am eighteen and a virgin.

$$\lightning$$

It is hard to believe I was ever this naive. It embarrasses me to admit I bought into Professor B.'s promises. But there was a dream I had hatched that my life would play out exactly like this. My talent was undeniable and would be recognized, and here comes Professor B. with an official acknowledgement of it.

I was not physically attracted to Professor B., but I was not sure what physical attraction was supposed to feel like either. I had had just one boyfriend before college and the furthest I had gone was second base. A sense of confused hope monopolized my thoughts.

When Professor B. warns me not to say anything to anyone about how he is going to mentor me to stardom, I feel special and in on a thrilling secret. As Professor B.'s chosen one I am no longer perplexed in acting class. I have natural talent that simply needs nurturing.

I have made it to college and adulthood. Anxious and eager to recreate myself, I believe, at first, that Professor B. is an ally. Now something, my soul perhaps, perhaps the witty and resourceful side of me, flashes a warning to proceed very carefully.

⚡

When the semester ends and the summer break is about to begin, Professor B. gives me a special assignment to work on—Nina's monologue from Anton Chekhov's play *The Seagull*. He explains he will secure auditions for me in the fall and for those I need pieces to display my acting ability. He dog-ears the page in my monologue book and makes me promise to return to him with the speech well-rehearsed.

That summer I work as a counselor at Camp Blue Bay. I use my days off to sit under a lone tree in the middle of the athletic field to work on the monologue. It is hot, mosquitoes buzz around my ears, yet I perch on a towel under a tree surrounded by dry grass all by myself and read and reread these words: "I am the seagull. No, that's not it. I'm an actress, that's it."

I do my best to comprehend what Nina means when she says those lines, but I do not have a clue. I try to rewrite the lines in my own words: "I'm a bird but I'm not a bird. I'm an actress. An incredible actress, but I keep fucking up because I'm a crazy person." I attempt to conjure up the skills I have learned in acting classes to put meaning behind the sentences, but I cannot connect anything together. On my one day off a week I could be lying on the beach taking in the sun or deep into an afternoon nap in my bunk, but I do not want to disappoint my mentor.

⚡

At the beginning of the fall semester I walk to Professor B.'s office and am about to knock when the door opens and out flies Mary Elizabeth, a senior theatre major. She sneers at me and sidles down the hall. With a swish of her hips she looks back at me before turning the corner. I am still staring after her when Professor B. steps out, smoothing his hair.

— Gosh, you look beautiful today. Come inside.

Professor B. puts his hand on my arm and pushes me toward the inside of his office. He quickly locks the door behind him.

— How I missed you.

Professor B cannot wait. He grabs me by the shoulders and kisses me. His mouth smells stale. I pull away and attempt to control the direction we are heading.

— Should we work on my monologue today?

— What monologue?

— Nina from *The Seagull*. My audition piece, remember?

— YES! Of course! The audition. That. We'll work on that next week.

— I have it memorized.

— We have to talk about something first and I want you to be honest with me.

— What is it?

— I want to talk about us. We can't go on meeting in this office all year. There's a place I know of. It's over in the next town. Do you understand?

— Yes.

— Good. Next time I'll bring the details and we can meet there.

He is anxious, reaches out to me with sweaty hands. He grabs me in a desperate embrace and we kiss again. I break free and reach for the door. When I am just a few short steps away, I hear him call after me.

— This is about your future. See you tomorrow.

I am the seagull. No, that's not it.

Red flags, red flags, red flags are all I see as I wheel it down the hallway. Professor B. completely forgot the monologue he assigned me. Red flag. Professor B. wants to meet me at a motel outside of town. Red flag. This does not feel right. Red flag.

Hope and disbelief and low self-esteem cover red flags, make them almost impossible to see. Maybe he did not forget the monologue. What if he is in love with me? Who else will champion my career?

The red flags melt away as an unpleasant realization rises. I might be the last virgin left on campus. I make a quick and final decision to visit the campus health clinic for birth control. Thank you, Girl Scouts, for two words of wisdom I have not forgotten: be prepared.

⚡

The receptionist at the health center informs me I cannot get birth control without being examined by a gynecologist. The doctor is male, and while I am completely humiliated by having to stick my feet up into stirrups and have a spotlight directed between my legs, I realize I will never have sex if I do not go through with this. I turn my head to the side and stare into the corner of the room.

— When are you getting married?

— What?

— When are you getting married?

— Married?!

— Yes, you are getting married, aren't you? That is why you're here?

— Sure. I mean yes. I'm, ah, getting married next month.

— Well, you're going to have to come back for an operation before then.

— Huh?

— I need to perform a surgical procedure before your wedding night. You'll bleed to death otherwise. Make an appointment for next week. In the meantime, here's a prescription for the pill.

WHAT? Exiting the clinic, I try to make sense of everything I just experienced, but all I can do is cry. I have never heard of anyone having to have an operation before sex. Not only am I the last virgin on campus, I am also a freak of nature.

⚡

I do not meet Professor B. at a motel. I tell him exactly what the doctor said. He is fine about it, grumbles something about how my health is, of course, a priority. I sense disappointment in his voice mixed with a touch of suspicion. I mean, really, an operation? Never heard that one before, I imagine him thinking.

I stay away from Professor B.'s office after that. He never mentions my career again. Very soon after this I begin to date a guy from my acting class. We go out for a few months and one night have sex. I do not bleed to death. I do not bleed at all.

Professor B. gives me a B in Acting. In all my years at SUNY Brockport I play just a few very small roles in the theatre department's mainstage productions. I am never cast as the lead. Granted, they do not produce many plays with female leads. In my senior year I decide to stage and star in my own production. With fellow classmate Joanne O'Connor, I produce *Save Me a Place at Forest Lawn* by Lorees Yerby, a one-act play about a deep friendship between two octogenarians. I go to a nursing home and interview women as research. Carefully dissecting the script into thoughts and moments, I invent my own acting technique. Our production impresses both students and faculty and goes on to a regional festival. When we graduate, both Joanne and I receive the theatre department's highest acting honor—the special award for performance.

$$\notin$$

I fill the prescription for birth control the doctor at the health clinic gives me. The pill causes headaches so intense I have to lie flat on my bed for hours with my eyes shut. Each morning I wake up nauseated. During the second month on the pill everything makes me sob: Nixon is impeached, Burger King is closed, "Kung Fu Fighting" is on every channel on the radio. During the third month on the pill I am convinced I am going crazy.

One afternoon I browse the selections in the Main Street bookstore in downtown Brockport and pick up a copy of *Our Bodies, Ourselves,* first published 1971 by the Boston Women's Health Book

Collective and written for women seeking information about their health. I learn the pill can have very bad side effects for some women. I throw my pills away and research alternative methods of birth control. Soon afterwards, I monitor my ovulation cycles by charting my basal body temperature and use the information to avoid getting pregnant. Eventually, I get a diaphragm.

Our Bodies, Ourselves shoves me into feminism. I begin to examine my life with the filter of my gender firmly in front of all the experiences I have had. Everything from the world of blah to the line, I-am-going-to-make-you-a-star, makes sense to me now.

What if I make it a point to live my life conscious of the filter of gender? What will my life be like? Will I be able to harness the inner power of my sex and never again give myself away or let others determine who I am? The answer is as dull and as steady as a menstrual cramp. You bet I will.

I am a feminist, that's it.

Whatever happens to me will be what I choose to happen. Whatever I want I will go out and get. The universe can step aside, because I will be the creator of my world.

I graduate, move to New York City, for six weeks live hyperaware of the inferior status my gender has placed me in, and push against it with all my might.

Then I meet Bill.

7

1978, NEW YORK CITY

I AM WALKING ALONG FIFTH AVENUE in my straight-legged black velvet jeans, a sheer tunic top with a black camisole underneath, and a pair of four-inch heels. Around my neck dangles the rhinestone necklace, circa 1942, I swiped from Mom's jewelry box. My hair is a mass of blonde cascading past my shoulders in soft curls. I reach into my black vintage evening clutch, pull out a bullet of Revlon lipstick, and apply a double dose of Fire & Ice to my lips. With a deep breath I inhale the Magie Noire perfume dabbed to my throat before I left my apartment. I am in perfect sync with New York City.

⚡

—For your twenty-fourth birthday I am taking you to La Côte Basque, Bill says to me over the phone. Meet me there.

La Côte Basque is the swankiest and only French restaurant I have ever been to. Bill grabs my hand, pulls me into the vestibule, greets in perfect French the grey-haired maître d', who fingers my elbow gently and whisks us both past a huge bouquet of fresh flowers and into a dramatic red room. Tiny lamps perch atop a dozen tables occupied by women in pearls and men in dark suits, who stop their quiet chatter to stare at us. Suddenly aware of the girly-girl power of my youth and beauty, I sweep my blonde hair from my right shoulder to my left to sustain our surprising command of the room. A waiter pulls out a table from the banquette. I step in, twist my body at the waist, and gracefully ease myself onto the leather bench. With an inhale that elongates my spine, I poke my chin up to look at Bill, who smiles. He grabs my hand. I sense all eyes are on us still.

Any memory of the era of low self esteem is firmly pinned underneath the spike of my heel with a sudden burst of confidence. In touch with the intensity my gender can radiate, perhaps for the first time, I let it gush like a *New York Post* headline: "Gorgeous Nobody Scores Date with Handsome Somebody."

— Une bouteille de Château Lafite Rothschild 1967, s'il vous plaît, Bill says, still looking at me as he sits in the chair opposite mine.

— I am going to share the things I love with you, his silky voice growls.

— I'm not sharing you at all, is my quick reply.

He laughs.

— I love it that there are things you've never experienced I can give to you.

— Thank you.

— Would you like your birthday gift now?

— Isn't this it?

— We are going to have this exact meal again, except the next time we'll be dining in Paris.

I almost blurt out a vulgarity but catch myself and quickly look around to make sure I pulled the words back into my mouth before being discovered.

— I'm taking you to Paris.

Paris? Paris? Like in fucking France?!

— That'll be swell, Bill. I can't wait.

Did I just say "swell"?

— I am going to teach you about life.

— Good. Fine. Sure.

Who cares, I'm going to Paris!

He orders foie gras, salade de crabe et homard, mignonettes de boeuf bordelaise, and, to start, Beluga caviar. He pulls a soft pack of Winstons out of his jacket, flicks his wrist three times until a few filtered ends peek out. I reach for a smoke and make a mental note.

Get a cigarette case for Paris.

He reaches across the table for my hands, presses the joints of my fingers together, and mashes them with his thumbs. I slip off my heels and run my toes under his pant leg. He tilts his head upward for a moment and then pushes his face close to mine.

From the dark corners of the room a huge trolley emerges. Sitting on top is the biggest oval tin I have ever seen. The tin is cradled in crushed ice, surrounded by four waiters and opened with a flourish. Three tablespoons of glistening black pearls are lifted onto a plate and placed in front of me. A waiter begins to demonstrate how to dollop a scoop of caviar onto a toast point using a mother-of-pearl knife when Bill waves him away. Bill takes my knife, spreads caviar onto a triangle of bread, and garnishes it with crumbled egg yolk and onion. With the toast perched atop his left hand, he moves it across the table. It looms above the red tablecloth, illuminated by the tiny lamp to my right, and stops to hover over my home-manicured nails.

Jesus, don't let me drop the caviar.

With both hands I seize the toast as delicately as I can with both forefingers and thumbs.

Goodbye nameless girl from Long Island who grew up eating piss clams steamed in Schlitz.

— Château Lafite Rothschild 1967, monsieur?

One of the waiters is cradling a dusty bottle and presenting it to Bill. He nods his approval. The waiter backs away, smiling.

— I ordered a special bottle of wine. You'll enjoy it. To be here with you . . . Bill trails off.

— What is it?

— Nothing. Except you are everything to me. Do you know that?

— As you are to me.

Who am I, Shakespeare, now?

— Tell me you know that.

— Of course I do.

Something serious and sad has made a swift invasion of Bill's spirit. He drops his chin.

Shit. Something is really wrong.

A waiter appears like a stealth ninja with the same bottle of wine semi-covered with a white cloth. He carefully slices the foil from the top of the bottle, snaps open a corkscrew, and in four swift twists pops out the cork.

Bill pulls himself together, smells the sample the waiter has poured for him, then sips from the glass. His somber mood instantly turns rapturous as he offers me his glass.

— Smell it first.

I take a ladylike sniff of the glass bowl.

— Cherries and chrysanthemums.

What the heck do chrysanthemums smell like?

I smile, laugh a tiny little bit, and then tip the glass up to pour the ruby liquid over my tongue.

Jesus, don't let me spill the wine either.

A sliver of self-assurance punctures my brain as the wine sashays against my palate. A different waiter brings a tall candle to the table, lights it, and places a wide-bottomed glass carafe next to it. Then he holds the neck of the wine bottle over the candle and carefully empties the wine into the carafe. During this process the two waiters stare at the candle and whisper back and forth to each other in French. When the bottle is almost empty it is whisked away.

Bill leans in and kisses me.

— You are so, so fine, he says as he once again reaches across the table for my hands.

I grin, blush, and feel euphoric. A woman's voice sings something in French.

Plaisir d'amour ne dure qu'un moment.

Bill's eyes click from sparkles to tunnels of despair.

— What is she singing?

— She sings about love. It lasts only for a moment.

— Maybe for some.

Bill does not hear me. Instead he says something unfathomable.

— I am afraid I will lose you.

You cannot be serious. I will never leave you. How can you not know that!

— You will never lose me, Bill. I am yours.

My words float into the air. He does not know the depth of my devotion, or maybe he just does not believe me. I brace my right foot against Bill's knee and slide the other over the top of his shoe. I pull his hands toward mine, inch my own hands up his arms until they grip his elbows. I lean my body forward, push my lips into his. The salt of the caviar and the fruit of the wine mingle. The flickering table lamp lights up our closed eyes and groping fingers.

I feel the strength of my kiss nail him down, return him to me. I control the situation, shape its outcome with the clean and focused force of my womanness. He surrenders, believes, understands I am completely his.

This is too bitchin' good to be true.

⚡

Regardless of how it was taught, the exposure to the work of Meyerhold and Grotowski leads me to explore and fall in love with experimental theatre. When I arrive in New York I know exactly the kind of actor I want to be, and so, soon after I take up residence on 19th Street, I wander south to the arty enclave of SoHo, find 33 Wooster Street, and ring the buzzer.

— Yes?

— Um, hi! I would like to get involved in the kind of theatre that you—

— What? Speak up. I can't hear you!

— Do you need an intern?

— Who is this?

— I just graduated from Brockport. You did *Mother Courage* there last year. I saw all three performances.

— Wait a sec. I'll be right there.

After a few minutes I hear someone galumph down the stairs. The lock clicks, the door swings open, and a woman pokes her head out, her eyes squint at the sun.

— Yeah, hi. I really like the Performance Group and was wondering if you need any help?

— Come upstairs.

We climb two very steep flights to a rehearsal space on the second floor. Willem Dafoe lies on a cot in the corner reading a book. He does not stir as we walk past him toward a dark corner of the room.

— Watch your step, and don't hit your head on that beam in the ceiling, warns Debby Locitzer, the Performance Group's executive director.

I follow Debby into an alcove office. She offers me a seat and gives me a short rundown of the current work of the group, then asks me about myself.

— I just graduated from SUNY Brockport with a degree in theatre. You toured *Mother Courage* there last year. It's the reason I'm here. I would love to do theatre like that.

— Well, we're in the process of opening up a new space next to the Performing Garage. Did you notice it when you walked by?

— You mean George's Diner?

— It's not really George's Diner. It's the environment for *Cops,* our next show. Jim Clayburgh is installing it and we could use some extra hands. Give me your information and then go downstairs and introduce yourself. He'll tell you what to do.

↯

The Performance Group, led by Richard Schechner, was the leading creator of environmental theatre, productions where the lines between the performance space and audience space are deliberately vague. I was greatly inspired by their touring production of Brecht's *Mother Courage and Her Children* when it came to SUNY Brockport in the '70s. Loaded into our black box theatre, the audience sat on and below scaffolding that surrounded a central playing area. The actors scrambled all over the space, including places where the audience sat, nudging them out of the way to play their scenes. The production zipped along with tightly choreographed scene changes, mini-spectacles unto themselves. The closeness of the performers, the physical commitment of the actors, the way the entire production enveloped me inside of it stayed in my mind. *I could do that,* I remember thinking as I watched a very pregnant Joan MacIntosh, as Mother Courage, grunt and strain against the ropes and pulleys that were an intricate part of the set.

The day I rang the buzzer at 33 Wooster Street I became an intern for the Performance Group. I swept the floors of the Performing Garage, painted scaffolding, and eventually was hired part-time as an administrative assistant. The most thrilling of all of my duties, however, was as a member of the stage crew of their production of *Cops* by Terry Curtis Fox.

⚡

Under the streetlamp on the corner of Wooster and Spring Streets in SoHo, I light up a cigarette. I check my watch. It is 8:30 in the evening. Two blocks away, above the door to George's Diner, a single light bulb suddenly glows white. There it is, my cue. I stomp out my cigarette, pick up the handles of the wheelbarrow beside me, and roll it into the middle of the street. My finger flips a switch on and the whirly light rigged to the bottom of the wheelbarrow bed flashes white and red, rotating slowly before picking up speed. As it whips around and around, I look down Wooster Street, check to make sure no cars are coming in either direction. Then I turn on the other contraption inside the wheelbarrow, the siren.

I pick up the handles of the wheelbarrow, inhale, and begin to run as fast as I can down the middle of the street. The siren is connected to the wheel of the wheelbarrow, so the faster I run, the louder the siren is. SoHo is usually deserted at this hour, but I slow down anyway as I cross Broome Street. The window of George's Diner in my sights, I slow to a jog, then to a walk, before coming to a complete stop, my whirly light focused directly into the frosted window and onto the environment of *Cops*.

After a few seconds I flick the siren off. Willem Dafoe, from the crawl space under George's, shouts into a bullhorn:

—This is the police! We have the building completely covered! Come out with your hands on top of your head!

I hear Stephen Borst, Ron Vawter, and Timothy Shelton shout at each other from inside George's. Then gunshots and silence. The performance is over.

After the audience files out, I roll my wheelbarrow rig inside the Performing Garage and stow it underneath a scaffold.

Spalding Gray and Liz LeCompte pass their blood-spattered costumes to the stage manager, who dumps them in a tub of soapy water. As the rest of the crew mop up the streaks of fake blood off the set, I step out from under the scaffold just as Spalding Gray emerges from backstage.

— Hi.

— Hey. Thanks for helping us with the show.

— I'm Donna.

— Spalding. Nice to meet you.

— I saw you in *Mother Courage*. You did it at my college. It was great.

— Did you study theatre in college?

— Yes.

— What did you study?

— Acting.

— Did you like the program?

— Not really. I'm learning a lot more here.

— College of the streets.

— Wheelbarrow acting technique.

— It's a great effect.

— People come up to me after to ask how it works.

— Don't tell them. How easy it is, I mean. Might spoil it, you know? Well, good night. See you tomorrow.

— Sure.

I watch Spalding walk away with the other cast members. I imagine myself in a performance, acting alongside Spalding and Ron Vawter, Stephen Borst, Tim Shelton, and Liz LeCompte. I will be the downtown complement to Bill's commercial success.

I throw on my jean jacket, step out onto Wooster Street, and head for the subway. Post-performance joy creeps into every joint in my body and I begin to skip and leap up the block.

⚡

Here is how I will become a great artist in New York City. It begins at my desk, a drafting table left behind by the previous tenant and attached to a wall of my tiny room. On the drafting table I lay out the road I will travel toward self-expression.

Stacks of newspapers and magazines I must read are piled on top in order of date. The *Village Voice* and *Backstage* are most important. In the *Voice* I circle reviews of shows, exhibits, dance performances, and films I believe will influence my artistic style in a profound way. Auditions in *Backstage* I assume I am right for are cut out and taped into a notebook. Next to the notebook is my datebook. A sample page might list a morning time of a dance class, an evening time of a performance or film screening, and a shift at Jimmy Day's or the Performing Garage. Days off might be completely blocked out with "write" written across them. On the right of the table are printouts of dance class schedules at Alvin Ailey's, Zena Rommett Ballet School, and Robert Audy Tap. Thumbtacks hold a calendar to a bulletin board on the wall above the desk; surrounding it are inspirational quotes and photos of artists I admire—Antoine Artaud, Martha Graham, Jack Kerouac, Judith Jamison.

The drafting table has no stool, so I stand at the desk organizing the days of my artistic life, sketching a personal plan of self-education any performing-arts conservatory would envy.

It is via this plan, in a small ad in the *Village Voice,* that I find out avant-garde theatre pioneer Richard Foreman, founder and artistic director of the Ontological-Hysteric Theater, is casting his first movie, *Strong Medicine*. Foreman's complex and theatrical style is exactly the kind of signature work I itch to make. Auditions for the movie are held in his SoHo loft.

I join the line of actors on the sidewalk with my picture and résumé in hand. Eight at a time, we are led up the stairs and into a large room. Foreman sits in front of us, looking intrigued and intense. In order of our standing, he asks us our name and where we are from. As I answer his questions he makes a sketch of me in a notebook resting on his lap. The "audition" lasts all of five minutes.

I am cast! It is only in the ensemble but I am cast! For one week I will be an experimental theatre actress filming in an abandoned hotel across from Duffy Square on West 46th and Seventh Avenue. Pay is subway fare plus lunch. I have to provide my own costume (pastel-colored party attire).

On the first day of shooting I arrive ready to go in a spaghetti-strapped blush-colored party dress. I report to makeup and have my face dusted with a layer of fine pale pink powder. I pick up a conical gold party hat the makeup artist has given me to wear and join the other members of the ensemble, women in green, blue, and yellow, men in dark vintage suits and ties. As I follow them to the set I begin my acting preparation by pulling my face into the best avant-garde, nonchalant, neutral look I can invoke.

The hotel is dusty and dank but on the second floor a ballroom has been cordoned off with black stage drapes. The scene I will be shooting is a birthday party for Rhoda, and we, the ensemble, are her party guests.

Rhoda is the protagonist in most of Foreman's plays and now his first feature. She is always played by the same actress, Kate Manheim. Also wearing a party dress, she stands on the set in the middle of the other principals. They include Ron Vawter of the Performance Group, the actor and writer Wallace Shawn, Mabou Mines founder David Warrilow, E. T. Kirby (my college professor), and his twin brother Michael, the then-editor of the *Drama Review*. I realize I am in the middle of experimental theatre royalty. I say hello to E.T. and Ron, who introduce me around. The assistant director instructs us to gather in the middle of the set as Richard Foreman enters.

Foreman is a quiet, smoldering presence. He does not shout or call out directives, preferring to work with actors individually or in small groups. He speaks almost in a whisper, his sad brown eyes convey a soft shyness. I feel a kinship with him immediately.

My avant-garde acting prep must have impressed him, because the first day he asks me if I can wear a blindfold for the next scene. I don a blindfold and kneel next to the overstuffed chair where Kate Manheim sits. My profile is in every shot. The next day Foreman asks if I can walk backwards into the shot. Of course I can. He asks more and more of me. Could I lean against this rail? Can I stand up when Rhoda approaches? Could I ask Rhoda for her autograph? My confidence grows. While I have no lines, I feel an important part of the film.

When I am not in a shot, I sit on the sidelines and watch. Lunches are spent talking to Ron Vawter, who draws me into conversations with Wally Shawn and David Warrilow.

I am young and eager and consider my job, a member of an acting ensemble, as a great opportunity. Every minute I am either in a scene or observing the process of filming from the sidelines. My brain is a creative container, and this experience gets stored inside, saved for later use.

The start date for Bill's feature film is delayed and delayed and he can do nothing but wait. Every night after the day's shooting wraps I go uptown and share my experiences on the set of *Strong Medicine* with him. On my last day of work he stops by the set to watch a few setups.

Toward the end of filming I wake up to find a note from Bill on the kitchen counter. He writes that he is proud of and confident in me.

I feel the stars are syncing up. In every aspect of my life, I am on my way.

⚡

It is time for Bill to meet my parents. My father picks us up at the Sea Cliff train station, drives the long way back to the house, down Prospect Avenue via Cliff Way, and stops at the bottom of the hill to show Bill Roslyn Harbor. My sweet, reserved dad gently answers Bill's questions about fishing in the Long Island Sound and lights up when Bill points out a good-looking cutter. My dad is a sailor and so is Bill. They hit it off right away and I am relieved.

We arrive at the house I grew up in, the house on Shore Road. Mom is at the side door and throws it open, her melodious voice belting out a strong "hello." She greets Bill as she does every stranger who comes to visit us, with a jaunty hug and kiss.

Dad takes Bill through the house, a house he built, showing him the tongue-and-groove cabinetry and fieldstone fireplace. Mom points out family photos featuring my sister and me in polka-dot leotards and shiny black tap shoes. The rest of the family arrives: my sister Dynie and her husband; my brother Ken and his girlfriend. My brother Ray would have been there, but he now lives with his family in another state.

We take our places around Dad's handcrafted dining room table and tuck into mom's lasagna. Bill offers up just the right amount of compliments to each dish and takes care to involve everyone in a buoyant conversation full of laughter. In ten minutes he is completely comfortable. It feels as though he has always been a member of the family.

At the end of an hour of stories and puns, my dad does what he always does when a guest has come over for dinner. He reaches behind him into the liquor cabinet and draws out a bottle of 140-proof plum brandy. While Mom clears the plates and slices up the apple pie, Dad pulls out a shot glass and pours Bill a shot of slivovitz.

It is Dad's big chance at a joke. Previous unsuspecting boyfriends, girlfriends, college buddies, and even the local priest have fallen for the offer of something to sip on at the end of a meal. No one ever suspected my soft-spoken dad would offer them something that tastes like turpentine. But before Dad can set up his joke, Bill spots the label on the bottle and proclaims not only a knowledge of but a love for slivovitz.

Bill accepts the shot glass without hesitation, and Mom enters with the apple pie just as he drains his glass with ease.

— Tell everyone what I gave you for your birthday!

Bill smiles at me, but I am busy trying to read Dad's disappointment and confusion at not putting one over on my new boyfriend.

— Um, I had caviar. It tasted like the ocean.

— Not that.

Bill stands and puts his napkin on the table.

— I'm taking your daughter to Paris.

Bill curls his arm around my neck and pulls me into a standing position. The flat silence is broken when someone claps their hands together, and all join in, looking unsure and slightly afraid.

— When? Mom blurts out.

Soon, Bill says, quickly sitting back down.

Dad refills Bill's shot glass. Nobody has ever had two glasses of slivovitz that I can remember. Raising his glass to us all, Bill toasts Mom's cooking and slugs back his drink. Mom slices up the pie and passes it around.

⚡

I think about not going, dream of waking up inside another body, one with arched feet, a supple spine, and an elongated neck. I know thoughts like those do an artist no good and so I find my way to the uptown subway and head for Alvin Ailey's.

All I can hear are drums. Congas, djembes, and bongos throb from behind the closed doors of every studio. As I walk the halls I match my steps to the changing beats.

The rhythms invade my skin, jiggle my nerve endings. I approach the studio I am searching for. Three other dancers are flopped along the floor in the hallway. I step over them and push my face up to the glass window in the door. Dancers in leotards, their underarms chalked with perspiration, gyrate across the length of the room. The drums thump out a final *whomp, whomp, whomp, whomp,* and the class is over. Applause cuts the air. Suddenly, there is silence.

The studio door flies open. Smells of sweat and rosin waft over the heads of the dancers as they exit the studio. I pull my dance bag close to my chest and brace against the wall as they file out past me. At the first opportunity I shove my way into the studio, toss my stuff in a heap against the wall, and scope out a good spot on the floor. Not in the front. Not too far in the back. Second row, middle side.

I check myself out in the mirror, make sure my leotard has not shifted into the wrong spots, pull it up at the hips and yank it down in the back. I lean over and scrunch my leg warmers over my ankles. Pointing and flexing my toes, I crack the metatarsals in my left foot and then my right.

At exactly three o'clock, Miguel Lopez, the Horton I (modern dance technique) teacher, floats into the room. He wears a topaz-blue unitard with a sweater slung over his shoulders. He wastes no time dictating the warm-up. The drummers bang a quiet, slow rhythm. On five, six, seven, eight, and . . .

With a straight back I hinge over from the waist on a count of eight. I do the same in reverse, repeating it four times. I try to feel my own energy extending outward, up to the ceiling and downward, into the floor with each round. The counts shorten to four counts down, four counts up; then two down, two up; one down, one up. We are halfway through the warm-up when Miguel stops us.

— I am missing *One Life to Live* for this? You are boring me! Do it again!

The drummers start. This time I convince my head to go a little deeper towards the floor, a little farther up to the ceiling. I see my spine as a river of water sloshing loosely against my rib cage. The flowing waters are frozen by the sound of Miguel's voice.

— You are moving but not dancing! It isn't just down and up and this way and that. It has no passion! No soul! You don't make love like this.

Miguel moves his hips a half inch forward and back.

— You make love like this!

He closes his eyes and thrusts his pelvis back and forth and back and forth. We all start to laugh. Miguel cuts us off.

— If you don't have passion you don't belong here. Now, once more or I am going home to watch my soap operas.

The drums begin again. I close my eyes and then open them. The water in my spine turns to mercury and rolls from my neck to my knees and back again. I perform the entire exercise without stopping.

There is silence. Miguel stares at us. We are not sure if he is pleased. There is not a sound in the room.

— You. Blondie. In the middle. Demonstrate.

Shit. Is he calling me out because I'm good or because I'm bad?

I try not to think about anything. In my mind I push away everyone in class, the mirrors, the drummers, and the door to the studio. The drumming gets louder and louder. My muscles are rubber inside my skin, bouncing up and down, up and down. I float on a river of spine up to imagine I can touch my head to the ceiling, down to imagine I touch my forehead to the floor. Over and over I repeat the same movement, breathing in to let the breath fill me up, exhaling it completely out before the next breath forms in my lungs. The music, my muscles, my mind are one. We beat out a message full of elation. I stick the end position and hold it.

Miguel looks at me, then at the class.

— That is how it's done. Now, everyone, across the floor.

$$\frac{4}{7}$$

The first director of *Altered States,* Arthur Penn, is replaced with Ken Russell. In New York City for a few days, he invites Bill to a dinner with some others involved in the movie. Bill asks me to join him.

We arrive late and take the only two seats left at the table. I pull out my chair and sit next to Paddy Chayefsky, who turns to me with a smile.

— What do you do?

— I'm an actress.

— Oh. Anything I might have seen you in?

I want, more than anything, to be able to say, *Yes, I was in this movie and that play,* but the truth is I run a wheelbarrow down the street for the Performance Group and just finished being an extra in a low-budget, experimental movie. I cannot push away the rising reality: I am the only amateur at the table. My gumption and belief in myself are about to fail. I muster up a quick, generic reply.

— I just finished shooting Richard Foreman's first film.

— I'm not familiar with Foreman. Tell me about him.

Chayefsky senses my discomfort and his question is an invitation to relax. Before I can answer, Bill begins a long-winded soliloquy to the entire table on Paddy's screenplay.

Saved by my verbose boyfriend, again. I am the perfect complement to Bill's need to speak. He is a brilliant orator and most everyone is hypnotized by his flowing ideas, including me. Intelligence and confidence are a combo I wish I could order up every time I feel like an outsider, but I cannot and thus am quite happy to have a front-row seat to the spectacular Bill show.

Tonight, Bill is not the only gladiator at the table with the gift of

Me.

First Day of School.

ishing with my dad.

Second grade. I was selected to represent the Sisters of Mercy in a procession for the Bishop. The habit was more uncomfortable than wearing a rubber gorilla mask.

My first tap-dance recital (with my sister, Dynie, on the right).

From Donna Kaz's personal collection

Brothers and sister. Clockwise from top, Ray, Dynie, Me, Ken.

From Donna Kaz's personal collection

Off to Girl Scout Camp—that's my sister photobombing me from the back of the car.

From Donna Kaz's personal collection

Home from college.
From Donna Kaz's personal collection

Save Me a Place at Forest Lawn with Joanne O'Connor, on left. We both received special honors from the SUNY Brockport theatre department for our performances.
From Donna Kaz's personal collection

Self-portrait taken in my loft after a shift at Jimmy Day's, 1977.
From Donna Kaz's personal collection

As Miss Casewell in *The Mousetrap*, South Jersey Region Theatre, 1978.

From Donna Kaz's personal collection

My first head shot.

Photo: Gerard Barnier

With Bill and Bats,
Malibu, 1979.

From Donna Kaz's personal collection

On location of *Altered States*,
Chihuahua, Mexico, 1979 (my
broken finger is still in a splint).

Photo by Morgan Renard

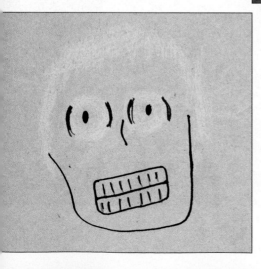

A drawing from a sketch book I kept in
Malibu, 1979.

From Donna Kaz's personal collection

With Blair Brown and Richard Jordan, Los Angeles, New Year's Eve, 1980.

From Donna Kaz's personal collection

With Carrie Fisher, 1978.

From Donna Kaz's personal collection

Charles T. Harper.
From Donna Kaz's personal
collection

n my studio at Yaddo, 1986.
rom Donna Kaz's personal collection

Mom.

From Donna Kaz's personal collection

Assistant director on the set of *The In Crowd*.

From Donna Kaz's personal collection

The only copy of "Oh! The Joys of Being a Woman Playwright" we could find still up the morning after we hired a crew to plaster them all over Times Square in 1999.

From Donna Kaz's personal collection

Masks on the dock at the Blue Mountain Center, 1999.

From Donna Kaz's personal collection

Me (aft) and Claude Cahun (fore) in a canoe at the Guerrilla Girls' Blue Mountain Center Retreat, 1999.

From Donna Kaz's personal collection

Getting mistaken for cast members from *The Lion King* while distributing stickers at the TKTS line, 2000.

From Donna Kaz's personal collection

The Art Cheerleaders

and the

GUERRILLA GIRLS

team up to protest sexism and racism on Broadway.
New York City
June 4, 5-8pm

Postcard announcing our collaboration with the Art Cheerleaders—Tony Protest, 2000.

The Art Cheerleaders cheering in front of Saint Patrick's Cathedral, Tony Protest, 2000.

Photo by Gertrude Stein

Protesters in paper bag masks—Tony Protest, 2000.

Photo by Gertrude Stein

Protesters in paper bag masks (rear view)—Tony Protest, 2000.

Photo by Gertrude Stein

Guerrilla Girls at the Tony Protest, 2000. I am on the far right.

Photo by Gertrude Stein

Group shot of the Tony Protest, 2000.

photo by Gertrude Stein

Marching to Radio City Music Hall, Tony Protest, 2000.

photo by Gertrude Stein

Me and NYPD Officer Purtell —Tony Protest, 2000.

Photo by Gertrude Stein

Some of the Guerrilla Girls On Tour! From L to R, Dorothy Parker, Frances Harper, Lisa 'Left Eye' Lopes, Anne Sexton, and Edith Evans.

Photo by Teri Slotkin

REDUCEcellulite BE *gone* DRY SKIN *vanish* **UNWANTED** facial hair**DIMINISH** STRETCH MARKS **FADE** *AGE SPOTS* **ELIMINATE***feminine* odor***LOSE*** weight ***DISSOLVE*** *belly* fat **ERASE***wrink* les ***REDUCE*** cell ulite ***be gone****d* ry skin***VANISH*** **unwanted** fa cial *hair* **DIMI NISH** *stretch* marks***FADE****ag* e spots **ELIMIN ATE***feminine* odor *LOSE* wei *ght***DISSOLVE***b* reduce *GONE**ERASE**FADE* vanish **VANISH**unwanted **dissolve***erase* fade **GONE** ELIMINATE **reduce** LOSE ERASE *Dissolve diminish* erase eliminateREDUCE **vanish** VANISH ***be gone* UNWANTED** **DIMINISH** reduce erase **eliminate** vanish unwanted **LOSE** diminish gone **ERASE** fade reduce **BE** **GONE** eliminate **FADE reduce** *unwanted gone* **DIMINISH** *dissolve* **DISSOLVE unwanted** LOSE **gone** eliminate ERASE fade *ReDuCe* diminish lose FADE reduce erase VANISH *dissolve* DIMINISH fade ELIMIN **ATE** unwanted reduce LOSE *Dissolve belly fat* ERASE fade **BE GONE** *lose* **DISSOLVE** FADE FADE *eliminate* **UNWANTED** *DISSOLVE* erase *VANISH*

I THINK SOMEONE WANTS ME TO DISAPPEAR

A public service message from: Guerrilla Girls On Tour! www.**GGONTOUR**.com

Guerrilla Girls On Tour poster —2011. Created as part of our play, *If You Can Stand the Heat: The History of Women and Food.*

With Richard Charkham. Married since 1993.

gab. Both Ken and Paddy challenge him with expatiations of their own. Ken's wife, Vivian, manages to shove a few sentences into the fray. As if sitting underneath a blitz of bullets flying back and forth at close range, I remain alert and invisible for the entire meal.

Hours go by. Bottles of wine appear and are drained. Suddenly, Paddy stands and announces he has to leave. He apologizes and quickly exits.

It is just the four of us left. More wine is ordered and drunk. Twenty minutes go by. Then, suddenly, Paddy reappears, standing behind the chair he just vacated.

— I wanted to say one last thing. I think Donna talks too much and she should give everyone else at the table a chance to speak. Good night, sweetheart. Try not to take over the table.

He leans over and kisses me on the cheek. Then he turns and goes.

All eyes at the table look at me and laugh. I laugh too. Now, perhaps Paddy ran into someone on his way out, was distracted for twenty minutes, and then returned to the table. But I believe he left the restaurant, walked down the street, and suddenly remembered what it was like to be young and nobody, sitting at a table full of confident and successful people, and the memory made him come back to give me something to never forget.

⚡

The radio alarm, tuned to WNYC, snaps on with the morning's news: *Three million dollars in cash has been stolen from the Lufthansa Cargo Terminal at JFK. FBI reports that it is the largest . . .*

Bill slams the radio off and drags himself into the shower. I reach across the bed for the phone and call my answering service, hoping to hear a message for an audition, but my message box is empty. I get up and pull his pink oxford shirt over my shoulders, pad into the kitchen, and put on a pot of coffee.

Bill steps out of the bathroom with a towel around his waist. He moves past me into the small kitchen, opens a cabinet, and takes four bottles of vitamins off the shelf. I shuffle into the bathroom, pull the shower curtain back, and turn on the water.

As the water runs over my body I remember the events of the night before and grin.

My shower is short. I grab the hot and cold knobs, cut the water off and reach for a towel from the rack. I rub the towel over my wet head and wrap it around my torso. In the living room, I pick up and put on my clothes from off of the floor. I glance over to see Bill with his hand on the open fridge door, drinking from a carton of orange juice. He flips the OJ carton closed, replaces it in the door, slams it shut, and looks at me.

— Where's my shirt?

— Over there.

I slink back to the bathroom, pick his shirt up from the floor, and hand it to him.

— It was on the floor?

— Along with all your other clothes.

— But you were wearing this and now it's on the floor.

— Sorry.

— I've got a bunch of meetings. Should last all day, maybe into tonight too.

— I'm going to dance class. Will you call me later?

He buttons up his oxford shirt and disappears into the bedroom.

I am just about to put my coat on when I realize I have not eaten. I step into the kitchen and pour myself a cup of coffee.

— Why are there two piles of vitamins on the counter?

— What did you say?

— I said is one of these piles of vitamins for me? The small pile?

— What kind of a question is that?

— These vitamins, Bill. There are two piles. Who are they for?

— How stupid can you be? Just how fucking stupid are you!?

— I'm just asking a question.

No answer. I walk over to the black leather Eames chair, a gift from his ex-wife who is not yet his ex-wife but I do not know that yet, and pick up my bag.

— Goodbye, Bill. I'm leaving now.

These are the last few seconds of my life with Bill, where all is well and everything is possible. As the clock hand brings this last moment to a finish, I stand solid with my two feet under me, next to a beautiful Eames leather chair, my bag across my shoulder.

He is a blur of pink flying at me from out of the bedroom, lunging for me, grabbing me by both of my arms.

— Hey! Watch . . . what are you doing?!

He jerks me in the direction of the door.

— Now is right. Get out. Get out right now!

— You're hurting me!

One hand lets go so he can throw open the door and push me with the other hand toward it.

— What are you doing!

He has me in the doorframe now and shoves me into the hall. He picks up his leg and kicks me hard in the thigh. I stumble back and sideways and bounce against the stair rail.

— Out of here, now! NOW!

He slams the door shut. I pull my bag over my shoulder and race down the stairs. Out on the street I walk quickly to the 72nd Street entrance to the 1 train.

Did he kick me? Did he just kick me out of his apartment?

I go over and over these events in my mind, replay them in slow motion from the moment I opened my eyes. There is a part I keep missing. A spot I cannot remember. It is the point where I made a mistake.

The subway is crowded and I am jostled to and fro. I pull the hood of my coat over my head and weep into it. There is something I did or said that made him angry. I go over and over every last detail I can recall, but I cannot remember what I want to remember.

I took a shower, then I said I was leaving. No, he took a shower, then he got the vitamins out. I asked him a question, what was it? I have to remember not to bother him in the morning. Why did I have to ask him so many questions?

The train empties out and I find a seat. As I sit down I feel a sharp pang in my leg. I ignore it, flip it quickly away, and cut to another, brighter memory. The feel of his shirt against my skin.

Before I can unlock the door to my loft I hear my phone ring and ring and ring and ring. I twist the key in the lock and race to the phone.

— Hello?

— Please come back. I need you so much to understand and forgive me for the things I do. You're the only one who understands.

— Oh, Bill . . .

— Tell me you still love me.

— Of course I do.

I hear him unravel on the other end of the line. He is falling to pieces.

— Please say you will come back.

— I'll be right there.

— Hurry.

I hang up and pivot for the door, a singular thought in my mind. I must return to him.

I dash into the hallway and fumble for my keys in my pocket. I jam the key into the lock and twist it once, check the door to make sure it is secure. I run for the elevator and push the down button seven times.

Come on! Come on, elevator!

The elevator doors open and I punch the buttons, hold down the "L" button until the doors close. Luckily the elevator does not stop and I reach the lobby. I blast through the glass lobby door and run down West 19th Street toward the train. I try not to think about anything. My muscles are rubber inside my skin, bouncing up and down, up and down. I breathe in, let the breath fill me up, exhale it completely out before the next forms in my lungs.

I'm coming. Hold on, I'm coming.

I race down the subway steps and jam a token into the turnstile.

Where is the train? Train, train, come now!

The platform, my muscles, my mind become one. I tap my foot on the platform. *Whomp, whomp, whomp.* The beats turn into a mantra. Train. Come. Now. Train. Come. Now.

The headlights of the uptown number 1 glare down the tracks.

Yes!

I get on the train, in an almost-empty car, and stand, my right hand grips a strap overhead. I am no longer crying. I am no longer questioning. I am passionate, following my dreams, bolstered by the fact that there is one man, one amazing man out there, who needs me more than he needs anything or anyone else.

Seventy-Second Street is a blur as I take the steps two at a time and bolt toward West End Avenue. I am in a race against the clock.

Coming to the rescue!

I push his buzzer three times, then three times again, our secret signal. The door to the vestibule clicks open and I am up a flight, then two when I see his apartment door swing open. I run into his arms as he slams the door behind me.

Everything is all right now.

All Bill needs is to be loved by someone exactly like me.

Everything is all right.

Exactly like me.

All right.

Me.

8

1998–99, NEW YORK CITY

Now I AM FORTY, AND THEN forty-one, and soon after that I find myself careening down a one-way off-ramp for the middle-age exit. A forty-something artist, my passion, drive, and creative impulses are unchanged. Yet I cannot avoid the outside message meant for me and every other forty-something woman artist—you are no longer relevant. Perhaps I never was.

The arts love to categorize and label but I resist definition. At this point in my life, I write plays. I also write both the libretto and the lyrics to musicals. I direct every one of my plays and musicals as well. When someone expresses a bit of interest in a play or musical of mine, their enthusiasm dissolves like a female condom when they find out I want to direct my own work. "No one can do both successfully" is what I understand to be the subtext when a literary manager or artistic director ends a meeting with "We'll be in touch."

Why should I have to flash my passport every time the writer in me has a hankering to travel to director-ville? As if being an artist means limiting instincts. As if I dangerously cross some rigid border when I write dialogue as well as visualize the movement of actors across the stage. As the creator of a work of art, aka maker of theatre, my instinct is to shape certain aspects of my play or musical from text to staging. I regard the creation of a piece of theatre as a frolicsome act; a house of mirrors the creative team travels through together until they reach the end.

Might this pooh-poohing of artists who refuse to be categorized be gender based? It is hard to tell. I know that plays by women have not been produced as often as plays by men, so it would make sense that women playwright/directors have also experienced a pushback.

In this theatre era, labels help to control and stifle women artists. We are often asked to identify ourselves as emerging or mid-career or established. We are either writers or directors, not both, and if we are both we are suspect.

All artists, regardless of gender, experience fear and isolation. But perhaps I would have more of a chance of being accepted in theatre if I did not try to straddle roles and present myself as a writer/director or a librettist/lyricist. Will a door that has not been opened to me be answered if I approach it with a more traditional knock?

Maybe. But I do not feel right about that.

As I grow older, I get bolder. There is less to lose. Or more to gain.

By 1998 I am often shocked by what comes out of my mouth. I have no problem speaking up. How did I become so audacious? When did I turn into someone completely different from the shy child, the moping teenager, the unsure young adult I used to be?

With very little time left to carve out a career, I apply to Sarah Lawrence for a Masters degree in theatre. They call me back three times for an interview before sending me an acceptance letter. I imagine they looked at my age and thought, *What is she doing here—she is too old to learn anything new.*

I admit, many of the classes I sit in on at Sarah Lawrence are ones I believe I could teach myself. I decide not to go to Sarah Lawrence. The Northeast Theatre Company in Scranton, Pennsylvania hires me as artistic director. Before I accept the job, I let the company know my role will involve making all artistic decisions for the company.

From now on I will speak up. However I arrived here, speaking up suits me.

In early 1998 the Guerrilla Girls decide a weekend retreat might be the perfect way to weave the energy of the new members with the wisdom of the old. Rosalind Franklin[10] offers to host it at her downtown loft. Handouts and agendas are copied and distributed dotted with words like "inspire" and "motivate." There are questionnaires to fill out, committees to join, and jobs to sign up for. An emphasis is placed on new projects, but even higher on the priority list is time set aside for us to get know each other as artists.

Perhaps because of the angry outburst between members on race and privilege at my first meeting, or maybe because of the apparent lack of organization, out of all the recruits only two of us return for the retreat. On the Friday evening of the weekend, everyone is offered ten to fifteen minutes to share the work they make as their real artist selves.

I enjoy watching the other Girls show slides and videos of their personal work but I have no interest in reading a scene from one of my scripts or talking about the production of *Who's Afraid of Virginia Woolf?* I recently directed. I am a new activist and want to get down to changing the world.

If the sharing of our personal work helps to meld the group, it is hard to say. Around twenty Guerrilla Girls attend this retreat and the same strident energy dominates. There is tension in the air too. With this big a group of women artists and individual egos, there is bound to be an ever-changing dynamic. I do not think much of it at the time. I concentrate on these facts: for a long time, Broadway and beyond have been almost all white and all male. Anxious to pitch ideas designed to attack sexism in theatre, I arrive at the retreat prepared to state my case.

Finally, Saturday morning arrives and future projects are up on the retreat agenda. In a circle of chairs, much like at my first meeting, the

---

10 Rosalind Franklin (1920–1958), British scientist and one of the discoverers of the DNA double helix.

Girls sit and voice their ideas. When it is my turn to present I stand up and admit I know little about the current art world. Instead, I want to attack what I do know, the theatre world.

I open my notebook and read what I have come up with, an idea for a visual work. Taking the famous paragraph found in every theatre program across the country, I twist the words to this:

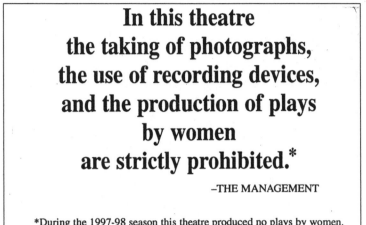

In this theatre
the taking of photographs,
the use of recording devices,
and the production of plays
by women
are strictly prohibited.*

–THE MANAGEMENT

*During the 1997-98 season this theatre produced no plays by women.

A PUBLIC SERVICE MESSAGE FROM **G**UERRILLA **G**IRLS

— That's fantastic!

Jane Bowles[11] bangs her hands together and gestures for me to pass the mock-up of my poster down to her.

— Let's print it!

Lorraine Hansberry[12] reaches for the poster.

— This is great. This is really, really great.

Gertrude Stein grins at me.

Hold on, women playwrights!

JANE BOWLES: How are you thinking of getting this out there?

---

11 Jane Bowles (1917–1973), America novelist and playwright.

12 Lorraine Hansberry (1930–1965), American playwright, author, and activist.

APHRA BEHN: Stickers? How about we put them in the toilet stalls of all the theatres not producing any plays by women.

LORRAINE HANSBERRY: Love it.

Wake up theatre world, where are the women?

GERTRUDE STEIN: Fabulous.

APHRA BEHN: The Roundabout and the Atlantic are just a few of the companies not producing any plays by women this season.

JANE BOWLES: Let's commit to completing this by the next meeting.

ALL: Agreed.

Everything is going to be all right now.

APHRA BEHN: Just like the art world, the theatre world needs us. Who else wants to attack the theatre world?

LORRAINE HANSBERRY: I do.

Everything is all right.

GERTRUDE STEIN: So do I.

CLAUDE CAHUN:[13] Count me in.

Guerrilla Girls are coming to the rescue!

We print "In This Theatre" onto Avery labels, six to a page, and distribute it to the Guerrilla Girls interested in our new theatre focus. In 1997–98, The Roundabout, Primary Stages, Signature Theatre, The New Group, the Atlantic Theatre Company, and George Street Playhouse are some of the theatres producing main-stage seasons of plays written entirely by white men.

If the show is at eight, I arrive at seven-thirty (so I can go to the women's room). Once inside a toilet stall I slip my hand into my purse, slide out a sticker, and quietly rip the backing off so no one can hear me. As I hold the virgin sticker in my palm, I kick the flush bar and slap the sticker

---

13 Claude Cahun (1894–1954), French writer, photographer, and performance artist who challenged gender and identity.

hard onto the wall of the stall at the same time. *Take that, you sexist theatre, you!* With a huge grin on my face I exit and make eye contact with the woman on line about to enter the stall I am vacating. *You are in for a treat.*

During intermission, I visit a different stall and put up another sticker. After the show I make one last trip to install a final sticker. All of this happens while my sympathetic Baboon Boy–escort stickers the men's room in much the same way. (We call men who assist Guerrilla Girl actions Baboon Boys, and while they help us carry out our mission, they are not considered official members of the group.) At least three stalls in both restrooms will be plastered with the Guerrilla Girl "public service message" by the end of the show.

The Girls obtain tickets to plays produced by these theatre companies either by purchasing them with our own money or with funds from the GGs. The most subversive way we sticker is when we volunteer to usher in exchange for a complimentary ticket. As ushers, we openly distribute programs, help patrons find their seats, and secretly apply public service messages to the insides of the toilet stalls.

As I participate in this first Guerrilla Girl theatre action I feel destructive, righteous, and omnipotent. A tremor goes through my core every time I slip the lock closed on a toilet stall and secretly smack another sticker into place. Each sticker is a monologue to a captive audience.

Hey, theatre-goer! Did you know you are supporting a company that produces no plays by women? They won't get away with it forever. Not while the Guerrilla Girls are around!

As each theatre mounts a new production in their all-white-male season, I return to the same bathroom stalls to continue the campaign. I have to suppress the urge to scream out an ebullient cry of "Victory!" when I see the remains of the sticker I had put up four weeks ago not completely scratched off.

(Hint: Avery labels are very hard to remove.)

We call ourselves the "theatre" GGs and carry out the action for the remainder of the season. Then we hear from an insider at one of these theatre companies. Our sticker campaign is brought up at an internal meeting.

Stopping the Insanity

A one-minute play

> LIGHTS UP on the offices of a sexist theatre company. MALE ARTISTIC DIRECTOR sits at his desk.

MALE ARTISTIC DIRECTOR

(pushing intercom button on phone) Phoebe, get in here!

> (PHOEBE, a bright and energetic young woman, enters)

PHOEBE

Yes, Your Artistic Dictatorship.

MALE ARTISTIC DIRECTOR

That list of plays for our next season I just gave you to type up. Any plays by women on that?

PHOEBE

No, sir.

MALE ARTISTIC DIRECTOR

Well, those damn Guerrilla Girls are at it again. Stickering the toilet stalls with their vile messages of equality. I guess we better put a play by a woman on that list.

PHOEBE

All right. Which one do you want to add?

MALE ARTISTIC DIRECTOR

I don't know. I can't think of any right now. What do you suggest?

PHOEBE

How about *The Women* by Claire Booth Luce? It's a classic.

MALE ARTISTIC DIRECTOR

Perfect. Then I won't have to deal with a living female playwright.

PHOEBE

Should I put it down instead of one of these plays by a white male?

MALE ARTISTIC DIRECTOR

Yes, yes. But don't tell anyone that I've given in to those masked cowards!

PHOEBE

Oh, I won't tell a soul.

(PHOEBE exits and goes to her desk. Dials phone and whispers into it)

PHOEBE

We can call off the sticker campaign. That's right. We strong-armed this theatre company with three-by-five paper stickers. When their new season is announced I suggest we take full and complete credit for its inclusiveness.

(PHOEBE hangs up and smiles.)

LIGHTS FADE TO BLACK

BOOM!

9

1978–79, NEW YORK CITY TO MALIBU

I AM A WAITRESS DATING SOMEONE on his way to becoming a movie star. I have to be on my way too. On the day after Thanksgiving, 1978, I take off my apron and quit Jimmy Day's. I am an actress and will find work as an actress. I swear I will.

Every week, as soon as it hits the stands, I buy *Backstage,* the weekly newspaper listing every audition in the city. Like most actors starting out, I do not have an agent to set up auditions for me, and so I pore over *Backstage* to find submissions and open calls. Submissions are listings for acting jobs describing the role and the production and where to send your picture and résumé. On my kitchen table are piles of large envelopes, eight-by-ten photos stapled to résumés, and a stack of stamps. I answer dozens of ads via U.S. mail, hoping someone will select my picture out of the hundreds they receive and call me in. A few days a week I attend open calls, aka cattle calls—a date, time, and place where anyone can show up and wait in line to be seen. Since every wannabe actress in town will be there, I get up at the crack of dawn to be at the start of the line. The first and only time I perform on a Broadway stage is the open call for replacements for the part of Rizzo in *Grease.*

Even though I arrive at 7 a.m., I wait four hours for a chance to sing. When my turn finally arrives, it goes like this:

STAGE MANAGER: When I say "go," walk out onstage, stand on the X mark, and state your name. The piano player will play one chord. When you hear it, start singing. Go.

(Walking confidently across the Broadhurst Theatre stage, I hit my mark.)

ME: Donna Kaz! (music chord, gulp, inhale, open mouth) *I could stay home every night . . .*

AUDTIONER: NEXT!

ME: (under breath) FUCK!

Four hours and seven seconds of my life as an actor melt away, a wasted chance.

I am not very good at auditioning because I am shit scared most of the time. The more I audition unsuccessfully, the more I doubt my abilities, the more I plummet back into the era of low self-esteem.

Part of my fear stems from this fact: I have no real training. Four years of undergraduate theatre classes aside, I am self-taught. By the end of college I believe in my ability to act, but my faith in my own talent comes up against this challenge when I hit New York City: Auditions are not acting, they are something else. I am not exactly sure what.

To better myself I read and reread *Audition: Everything an Actor Needs to Know to Get the Part* by Michael Shurtleff, and even sit in on one of his classes. Still, for me, auditions are nothing more than an awkward meeting of strangers. I so desire to be exactly what the casting people want, all I can think of when I walk into the room is, "Please, please, let's skip this part. Just give me the job already. I promise you I am precisely who you are looking for." Alas, no audition miracle/intervention occurs and so I launch into my one-minute prepared comedic monologue. But I do not know where to look—at the people in the room or above their heads? I do not know if I should sit or stand or how close or far away from the casting people I should I be. What if they stop me before I get to the really funny part? No matter what I do, the only thought in my head during my monologue is, CAST ME, CAST ME, CAST ME, CAST ME! As I think back on it now, I am a more than a bit relieved no one ever stood up and ran from the crazy, desperate actress before them.

⚡

— What are you reading?

   — *Backstage.*

— Never heard of it.

— You're kidding.

Bill is not kidding. He has been represented by an agent ever since he attended Juilliard.

   — It lists auditions. How do you audition, Bill?

   — What do you mean?

   — Do you have some trick you do to keep you calm?

   — That is my business. Don't ask me about it.

   — I was just . . .

   — . . . using me. Trying to use me.

   — No I wasn't . . .

   — Yes you were. That's all you want, isn't it?

   — Forget it.

Bill is alternately supportive and cold about my struggles to make it an as actress. The gap between our experiences as artists is already wide and grows wider each day. Yet the occasions where he places an arm across my back, pulls me in, and lets me know he believes in me, make all my sweaty, despondent interpretations of Portia's "quality of mercy" speech from *The Merchant of Venice* wax brilliant.

⚡

When I am not focused on my soon-to-be-career as a significant actress, I live the life of a struggling nobody. I accompany Bill to events he is invited to. We hear Luciano Pavarotti at the Met. I sit right behind Diana Ross. *Click, click, click.* We attend fashion week. I sit right next to Lauren Hutton. *Click, click, click.* After the runway show we go out to dinner with Carrie Fisher and John Heard. Bill's pal from Juilliard, Christopher Reeve, invites us to the premiere of *Superman.* At the screening we sit right behind Christopher and at Christopher's table for the after-party where Tom Selleck looks at me intently, convinced we have met before. *Click, click, click.* We are uptown, downtown, all over town at the hippest parties and restaurants, formerly miles out of my league. I have no problem fitting in as a legitimate member of the in crowd. I pass as belonging to this hip tribe because of who I am with. I pass because I know how to blend in. I pass because I am young and fresh and pretty and who does not like young and fresh and pretty? Yes, I can act. Oh yes, I can.

Acting or passing may be my gift, but I know nothing about networking, promoting myself, or how to use situations I find myself in for personal gain. I am deeply in love with Bill and I want to support him and his dreams. He is welcome to occupy center stage while I stand by rocking an inexpensive skintight dress, fake pearls, and blood-red overglossed lips.

Sometimes I am in a fairy tale, in love with a strong and handsome man who is just as much in love with me. Every waking moment we can carve out to be together, we do. It is the age of land lines. He finds pay phones and phones backstage and casting office phones to call me five, six, seven times every single day to repeat he loves me, in case I need a reminder. Or he gives me the numbers of rehearsal studios or his agent's office so I can call him. Not a day goes by where too much time passes without us professing our connected love to each other through the wires. I love him so much I feel physically incomplete without him, count the minutes until the next time we will be together. He writes me love notes and leaves them on my dresser, on my mirror, taped to his front door. I squirrel them away inside my coat pockets, finger the folded corners as I walk from subway platform to street to audition; the physical evidence of our most powerful love becomes my lucky charm. Every morning we wake up together, coordinate our days so the times when we must be apart are minimal. Each day always culminates in a glorious reunion of passion and romance. I cannot see a time when we will not be perfect lovers and forever happy.

Except when I *can* see that time. He is living his life a little bit more and I am living my life a little bit less. He needs me and depends on me and promises one day the tables will turn, the roles will be reversed, and he will be there for me. But now he cannot exist without my help. He travels an intense and demanding road and is often consumed by a deep, ominous dread, the origins of which confuse me. I hold his hand, do my best to guide him through. He grows to depend on me, worship me, resent me, hate me. He blames me for his funk, convinced he will fail and I will be the cause of his ultimate demise. No, no, I reassure him, but by then I have forgotten how we got here and cannot find the way back. So I wait for these gloomy moments to pass. They pass so quickly at first I soon forget they even happened.

The clock ticks down my life as an unemployed actress. A whole month goes by; my audition prospects turn lukewarm, then cold. Nothing in my monologues produce a positive reaction, so I substitute fear with anger. I tap into my inner bitch, and no matter what the audition calls for, every time I step inside an audition space I reach down, open my mouth, and rend the air with an earsplitting wail. I bank on the hope the world waits for an actress of my depth to let out the fury of female youth. Acting is screaming. I do not get one single callback.

Years later, when I sit on the other side of auditions, I witness many angry young women get into character and howl their way through monologues exactly like I used to. *You go, girls,* I think to myself, while secretly wishing I could give each one of them a hug and tell them it is going to be okay. *Let it all out, bitches, so the world can hear you. Roar out the music that is the ire of our gender.*

Eventually, I catch on that performing every monologue as if I am Medea may not be the best choice and master entering an audition room with confidence, presenting a firm handshake, and stating my name not so loudly. I find new and unique material that is upbeat and funny. I am prompt, organized, and professional. My head shots kill. My auditions get better. Still, I do not get cast.

$$\lightning$$

With my part-time job at the Performance Group, I am able to eke out a living. By now, the Performing Garage has four performance spaces and I see everything presented there from Theodora Skipitares to Charles Busch to Mabou Mines to all of Spalding Gray's *Three Places in Rhode Island.* The naturalistic works of Lanford Wilson and John Bishop as staged by Circle Rep are another source of inspiration. I fill notebooks with ideas for theatre pieces of my own, fusing the avant-garde and the naturalistic with movement, text, and song. Fellow graduates of the SUNY Brockport theatre department gather at my loft for informal rehearsals and to conceptualize what our own theatre company might one day look like.

I am a young artist in New York City—exposed to new work, conceptualizing a new form of theatre, associated with (if only by a part-time job) a theatre company I respect. I am also the partner to the most magnificent artist I know. Up ahead, a smooth path beckons. How lucky am I?

Better not spoil that luck. Better not. The love notes and the little gifts and the phone calls might dry up. Where is he right now? Is he with someone else? Better not ask him. He told you where he was. You must have forgotten. He comes home late, his wet hair reeks of an unfamiliar scent. Better not ask him why. Do not say anything to provoke. Best to be silent. Silence works until he is sick of your silence. What did I do? What can I do differently?

One night you drive out to New Jersey to meet his brother's family. You are nervous but you should not be. They love you.

One night you are invited for dinner with his stepfather and his family. You are nervous and you should be. You get into an argument just before you leave his apartment. When you arrive, he introduces you around and then abandons you smack in the middle of their swanky Sutton Place penthouse. You wish you could disappear, but you are at the table with everyone trying to make small talk, trying to enjoy the food served by the butler, prepared by the private chef. Everyone ignores you, especially him. You feel as if you are not even there.

It is Friday night and you make plans to spend the weekend with him at your brother's beach house. He rents a car and you drive south, head for the Brooklyn Bridge. As you slip in and out of the deserted streets of downtown Manhattan you turn to him and say something. Maybe you did not say anything. You cannot remember. What you do remember is lying in the middle of a street somewhere in SoHo. Two strangers hover over you, ask if you are all right. Did you fall out of the car? The door opened and you came flying out of the car. How did you fall out of a moving car? Why is the car stopped a hundred feet up the street? Is he waiting for you to stand up and run back to him? Just as you convince yourself he is waiting, you see something shoot through the air. It is the boom box you were bringing to the beach. It hovers directly over your head and seems to float there. It looks like a dangerous bomb that could fall right on you. You should move out of the way, but you are frozen. It crashes down in the middle of the street just next to you, busted up into a million pieces now. The two strangers run away. Now it is only you lying on the ground, watching him drive away. Somehow you make it to your brother's. You make up some excuse as to why he could not make it. You cry yourself to sleep trying to recall what you did. What did you do? The next morning he calls. He is sorry. He will never do it again. He takes the train to meet you. You pick him up at the station. He brings flowers. He brings a new boom box. You recognize him. He is the man you love. He promises he will never, ever, ever do what he did again. Do what? Do what again?

Love is an addiction. You cannot live without your love. You depend on each other, way past the point where it turns toxic and can kill you. You overdose on love, are rescued, revived, and dry out, only to repeat the same patterns over and over. You learn this much too late. Much, much too late.

⚡

Christmas is coming. I want to get Bill something very special, something that will be with him forever. He loves dogs. At the Bideawee animal shelter I find a litter of brown and black puppies. One little brown female comes to the edge of the cage and licks my fingers. I want to give her to Bill as a gift but I am unsure. What if I take her home and he does not want her? I decide to tell Bill about this little puppy, and as soon as the words are out of my mouth he jumps up and insists—no, demands—that we both immediately get in a cab and head for Bideawee to pick up his dog.

We bring her to my loft. Bill does not want to name her until he figures out her personality. After a few days he calls her "Bats" because she is high-strung and a little bit crazy. He is very gentle and patient with her. Bats and Bill bond with each other. The three of us feel like a family.

⚡

In 1979, Stephen Borst and Ron Vawter of the Performance Group offer a two-week workshop in performance at the Garage, and because I work there, they let me take it for free. The workshop is playful and Stephen and Ron create a nonthreatening environment whereby all ten participants are empowered to explore and have fun. For the first time I feel I am learning something about acting.

During the workshop, the Performance Group announces that *The Balcony* by Genet will be their next production, directed by Richard Schechner. I know Schechner from my backstage work on *Cops,* which he also directed. Schechner hopes to cast an ensemble for a workshop before the actual production and places a call in the *Village Voice* for actors. On a Saturday morning I, and about sixty other women and men, show up to try out.

Schechner's call is not the kind of audition I am used to. He asks all of us to stay for the entire day and to work as an ensemble. He will guide us through exercises exploring themes of power and sexuality. I so want to do well but it all feels a bit too much like working with Professor B.

Schechner instructs us, as a group, to improvise. To start us off he points to a woman wearing big, heavy-soled boots and invites her to begin. The woman steps into the center of the space stage and demands that we all lick her boots. Without even a moment of hesitation, a few actors leap to the floor and comply. Talk about commitment. *These guys will be cast,* I think to myself, followed by, *There is no way in hell I am licking anyone's boots.*

I glance up at where Schechner stands and see he is impressed. As tongues fly and slobber accumulates on the woman's boots, I decide to enter the exercise and try something else.

— Hey, everybody. What do you say we all . . . do something else!

— Lick my boots!

The woman stares at me and points to the ground. Uh-oh. This was a big mistake. Too late to back out now.

— Sorry, I didn't hear—

— You heard me! I said lick my boots!

— No. But thanks anyway.

The rest of the afternoon does not go any better for me. I feel isolated, prudent, and uncool. I am guarded and wary of the other actors and this blocks any hope I have of letting the performer inside of me out. At the end of the day Schechner pulls me aside to inform me he is very sorry but he does not think I have any talent. He says those exact words—"You do not have any talent"—as if he is letting me in on vital information that will save me the heartache of one more second chasing down a career in a genre I will never succeed at. Then, and almost as quickly, he offers me a part in the ensemble because, he explains, of all the work I have done at the Performing Garage.

I have no talent, but, what the hell, come be a part of the workshop because you swept our floors for free. I do not remember which I thought was worse—being told I was talentless or scoring a role on sympathy.

On the way out I run into Ron Vawter and tell him what Schechner said.

— Who cares what he said. You're going to come back, aren't you?

— But he thinks I'm no good!

— Fuck him. He offered you a part, now show him what you can do.

— Really?

A week later I join the other ensemble members at the first rehearsal. Also present is the woman wearing the big boots.

⚡

Bill flies to Los Angeles for a week to find a place to live during the filming of *Altered States*. He rents a 1950s bungalow right on the beach in Malibu, with the hope that it will be a welcome respite from the demands of the movie. He asks me to join him and live with him there when the movie begins. Of course I will, that is, if *The Balcony* workshop does not conflict.

The start date for *Altered States* keeps being pushed back, so Bill signs on to play the lead in Circle Rep's production of *The Runner Stumbles* by Milan Stitt.

Meanwhile, I continue to look for a paying acting job. I submit my head shot to the South Jersey Regional Theater and get a call to audition for two plays in repertory—Joe Orton's *What the Butler Saw* and *The Mousetrap* by Agatha Christie. Perhaps Schechner's words to me tear down the fear I have of not doing well, because for the South Jersey Rep audition I maintain an aura of nonchalance that makes me believe it is the best audition I have ever given. Sure enough, I get a callback.

When I return to read again for South Jersey, I do everything I can to suppress feelings of inevitability. I will not get this job just as I have not gotten any other jobs I have auditioned for. During the callback my gut tells me they want to cast someone who can act in both of the plays they are producing. I can tell the director, Paul Aiken, likes my work, but I also sense he is not convinced I am right for both shows.

After the audition I wait for the phone call—the call offering me the job. I have done everything I can. Dare I trust my sense that I did well? And then it comes. I am offered the role of Miss Casewell in *The Mousetrap* at the South Jersey Regional Theater. I am not hired for both plays, but I do not care because I am cast and will be paid for the very first time to act! I am, at last, an actor!

Even more fabulous is showing up the next day for rehearsals for *The Balcony* and informing Richard Schechner that unfortunately, I will not be able to continue in the workshop because I HAVE BEEN CAST IN ANOTHER SHOW!

⚡

On January 14, 1979, *The Runner Stumbles* opens.

On February 18, 1979, *The Runner Stumbles* closes. The following day Bill boards a plane bound for Los Angeles and preproduction work on *Altered States*. I promise to meet him there as soon as *The Mousetrap* show closes.

On February 25, 1979, I move out of my loft and put all of my belongings into storage at my parents' house on Long Island. I board a bus bound for New Jersey, arrive in Somers Point, and am picked up and taken to the South Jersey Regional Theater's company house, just a block from the Gateway Theater, where I will live for the next five weeks.

On March 14, 1979, I make my acting debut as Miss Casewell, a strange, aloof, and masculine woman, in the first performance of the South Jersey Regional Theater's *The Mousetrap*. Bill sends flowers and a telegram; his words evoke love and pride and a special instruction to enjoy my worth.

I do just as he counsels and every night rummage deeper into my memory to bring out the parts of me similar to Miss Casewell's inner life. The director is pleased, the audience responds; there is no need to convince myself anymore I have talent and can act.

On March 31, 1979, *The Mousetrap* closes. On April 1, 1979, I fly to LA. My plane lands at 8:45 p.m. I leap up from my seat as soon as the seat belt sign is off; my heart flutters beneath the fabric of the same pink party dress I wore in the Richard Foreman film. Weeks have gone by and I cannot wait to be in Bill's arms once again.

He is right there, at the gate, with a huge bouquet of flowers. We latch on to each other like magnets, our lips lock, our hands grope, our bodies behave as though deprived of essential nutrients only the other can provide. The rest of the world fades from view for our dramatic reunion, which we sustain for at least ten minutes. Everyone else has left the gate, collected their luggage, and are in cars headed for their destinations, but Bill has sat me down to look at me. While he looks he smiles and cries and kisses me and thanks me for coming, almost not believing I am really there.

Thirty minutes go by before I ask if we can leave. He remarks, for the umpteenth time, how beautiful I am. At baggage claim my lone suitcase revolves around and around on the carousel. Bill picks it up and leads me to his rented red Mustang in the parking lot.

Speeding up the 10 freeway, heading north, we dip into the tunnel that heads from Santa Monica to Pacific Palisades and zip along the Pacific Coast Highway. The blue-black ocean looks like a smooth blob of twinkling Jell-O under the slice of white moon. I roll down the car windows, let the sea air into my lungs as Bill grabs my hand and presses his lips to the back of it. We wind our way farther and farther from the guts of the city of Los Angeles, cross the Malibu city line, and arrive at our bungalow, where Bats waits for us. Here is where I will live, love, laugh, and cry for the next eight months. *The Mousetrap* will be my last and only paying acting job for decades.

10

1998–99, NEW YORK CITY

TAKE THE GUERRILLA GIRLS' THEATRE QUIZ

WHAT DO PRESTIGIOUS THEATRE COMPANIES HAVE IN COMMON?*

a. Latecomers are seated at the discretion of the management.
b. Their 1997-8 seasons included no plays by women.
c. Both of the above.

HOW MANY WOMEN HAVE WON A TONY FOR DIRECTING?

a. Twenty-eight.
b. Three.
c. Zero.

SINCE 1947, 50 PLAYS HAVE WON THE TONY. HOW MANY WERE WRITTEN BY WOMEN?

a. Women don't write plays suitable for Broadway.
b. How can you be nominated if you aren't produced?
c. One and one-half.**

ANSWERS: 1C, 2C, 3C

**Roundabout Theatre Company, Primary Stages, Signature Theatre Company, The New Group, Atlantic Theatre Company, and George Street Playhouse (to name a few.)

**Frances Goodrich (with Albert Hackett) for *The Diary of Anne Frank*, 1956; Wendy Wasserstein for *The Heidi Chronicles*, 1989 (no woman of color has ever won.)

GUERRILLA GIRLS THEATRE
CONSCIENCE OF THE ~~ART~~ WORLD

532 LaGuardia Place #237, New York 10012
Fe-mail: gg@guerrillagirls.com

AS APHRA BEHN, GUERRILLA GIRL, I attack the theatre world! The GG theatre committee (me, Claude Cahun, Gertrude Stein, Lorraine Hansberry, and a changing cast that includes Jane Bowles, Hannah Höch,[14] Hallie Flanagan,[15] Violette Leduc,[16] and others) gather in restaurants, coffee shops, or someone's apartment and devise ways to stick it to the sexists in theatre.

The stats are easy to obtain. A quick glance at a season brochure or the listings in *American Theatre* magazine and the *New York Times* unveils our next targets. When just four, five, or six of us gather it is easy to hunker down together and focus on output. As theatre artists we are experienced in the collaborative nature of theatre and work well as a team. Like witches stirring a cauldron of creativity, we add jokes and humor to the pot and stir until the persistence of inequity in the performing arts is so obvious, it is comical.

The days of carrying buckets of wheat paste, brushes, and black-and-white posters hot off the press, intent on blanketing every empty surface of SoHo with a public service Guerrilla message, are over. There are fewer blank spaces to poster, security is tighter, and our mission has expanded beyond SoHo. If we want to post visuals about sexism in theatre it makes more sense to poster Times Square. We try that, hire a group of college students to poster the theatre district in the middle of the night, but the next morning we find just one "Oh! The Joys of Being a Woman Playwright" poster flapping from a lamppost

---

14 Hannah Höch (1889–1978), German Dada artist and an originator of photomontage.

15 Hallie Flanagan (1890–1969), American producer/director, playwright, and director of the Federal Theatre Project.

16 Violette Leduc (1907–1972), French memoirist and novelist.

Oh! THE JOYS OF BEING A WOMAN PLAYWRIGHT!

•You're in control! **You produce your own plays because if you don't, they won't get produced!***

•You're special! **During Black History Month or Women's History Month your work receives at least one staged reading!**

•You're hot! **If you're under the age of thirty your career might last a few seasons!**

•You save money! **You don't have to buy evening gowns for all those awards ceremonies!**

•You live in the moment! **No need to obsess about your place in theatre history—you won't have one!**

•You don't fear failure! **Your breasts are the only things that will flop!**

*81% OF ALL PLAYS PRODUCED IN THE U.S. DURING THE 1998-99 SEASON WERE WRITTEN BY WHITE MEN.

SOURCE: *AMERICAN THEATRE* SEASON PREVIEW ISSUE, OCTOBER 1998

A PUBLIC SERVICE MESSAGE FROM **GUERRILLA GIRLS** CONSCIENCE OF THE *THEATRE* ART WORLD
532 LaGUARDIA PLACE, #237• NY,NY 10012
www.guerrillagirls.com

on 43rd Street. The rest have been ripped down by the expeditious Times Square cleanup crew.

We look beyond our previous schemes and hit on the Tony Awards, those celebratory statues honoring Broadway's best (so far mostly white men), as a perfect vehicle for the Guerrilla Girls to put a spotlight on our new mission. The 1998 Tony Awards are the American Theatre Wing's 52nd annual. In fifty-two years not a single woman has ever won a Tony for directing a play or a musical. Women and artists of color are not nominated for Tonys because they do not work on Broadway, where theatre artists earn some of the highest salaries.

If slapping up posters is passé, we place the "Take the Guerrilla

Girls' Theatre Quiz!" in the then-popular *In Theatre* magazine's special Tony Awards issue. A few of us even slip on our gorilla masks for Tony night and stand across the street from Radio City Music Hall, the venue for the awards ceremony. With other screaming fans we throw our hands up and shout at the arrival of each limo depositing Broadway stars just yards away. We do our best to tell whoever will listen who we are and why we are there. Our full-headed rubber masks stifle our voices and most mistake us for gimmicky actors trying to promote a new show. Shoved to the back of the pack, we give up and head home to watch the ceremony on television.

And then, for the very first time, a woman wins the Tony for best direction of a play *and* another woman wins for best direction of a musical. It is a grand slam for gender parity in theatre and we take full and complete credit for it.

We believe our ad in *In Theatre* pushed the issues of sexism in theatre just over the edge and into the mainstream. The Broadway community is finally paying attention. The Guerrilla Girls have changed American theatre!

CUE KARAOKE MUSIC:
("I Enjoy Being a Girl," from *Flower Drum Song*)
Everybody, it is time for a SING-A-LONG!
"WHEN YOU VISIT BROADWAY THEATRES
AND SEE ACTORS THAT SING AND TWIRL
IN SHOWS BY WHITE MALE DIRECTORS
YOU SHOULD CALL GUERRILLA GIRLS!"

The press snaps awake. Calls about the Girls' new foray into theatre come from Margot Ebling at the *Village Voice,* who interviews me, Claude Cahun, and Gertrude Stein. In her article, "The Guerrilla Girls Hit Theatre Sexism," she describes our sticker campaign aimed at naming theatres that are not producing plays by women. We talk about the marginalization of women in theatre and the labeling of plays by women as "women's theatre." Simi Horwitz interviews me and Lorraine Hansberry for *Backstage,* announcing that the Guerrilla Girls are now tackling the theatre world with humor and balls. Simi mentions a postcard included in the Guerrilla Girls' "Spy Kit," a paper bag filled with spy missions directed at galleries, museums, and now theatres we create for an exhibit entitled "Urban Encounters" at the New Museum. The postcard, addressed to those theatre companies not producing plays by women in their current mainstage seasons, reads . . .

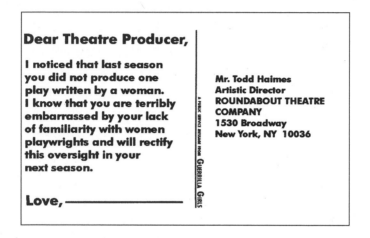

Dear Theatre Producer,

I noticed that last season you did not produce one play written by a woman. I know that you are terribly embarrassed by your lack of familiarity with women playwrights and will rectify this oversight in your next season.

Love, ───────────

A PUBLIC SERVICE MESSAGE FROM GUERRILLA GIRLS

Mr. Todd Haimes
Artistic Director
ROUNDABOUT THEATRE
COMPANY
1530 Broadway
New York, NY 10036

The Spy Kit reaches out to the theatre community and invites them to join us as "spies" and carry out guerrilla actions against discrimination in theatre. Join us they do. Some even write to us about it.

Hello Girls!

My name is Lisa McNulty, I am the Literary Manager of Women's Project and Productions, an Off-Broadway theatre that is devoted entirely to producing work by women (and one of the few theatres in New York unlikely to receive one of your brilliant postcards). I picked up a Guerrilla Girls Spy Kit recently at the New Museum and was bowled over. Does owning and using my Spy Kit make me an unofficial Guerrilla Girl?

All the best,

Lisa McNulty

Dear Lisa,

    Yes.

Love,

Aphra Behn

Soon after we receive this email, the Roundabout announces their 1998–99 season will include two plays by women: *Impossible Marriage* by Beth Henley and *The Mineola Twins* by Paula Vogel. They have not produced a play by a woman since 1986.

Wow, wow, WOW! We take full and complete credit for this as well. In my almost twenty years as a masked avenger Guerrilla Girl and Guerrilla Girl On Tour!, I have learned that it is important to celebrate the gains. They do not come very often. High fives and fist bumps all around.

In 1998 I also travel to my first Guerrilla Girl "Gig"—a presentation of Guerrilla Girl posters accompanied by two Girls who share the stories behind their creation. On the stage at Queen's University in Kingston, Ontario, I feel the energy and love of the audience. I relax just enough to stray from the script, improvise a few lines about the new work of the GG theatre committee, and get laughs. I am on a stage, acting again. For the next two decades I will perform, with confidence, on stages all over the world. Being a Guerrilla Girl provides me a rare opportunity: the chance to try out material in front of a different live audience each week and tweak it until it works. This teaches me volumes about playwriting and acting and connecting with an audience, all of which I fold into my own theatre-making.

In the spring of 1999 I am hired by a nearby college to direct a production of Jean Anouilh's *The Lark*. When only six students show up to audition for twenty parts, I write and direct an original play about Joan of Arc specifically for those six students instead.

Now the opportunity to stage the kind of theatre I have wanted to create is right in front of me. I move into an apartment on campus and take out every book I can find on Joan of Arc from the college library. During the day I write the play. In the evening I workshop the material with the four women and two men in the cast.

There is no theatre department at the college. I have been hired to expose the students, most of them math and science majors, to theatre. It is a perfect environment to experiment with the ideas on ensemble theatre I have been devising for years.

I toss in everything I have absorbed since moving to New York City, from my work with the Performance Group to all of the productions I witnessed at the Performing Garage and Circle Rep. I create a performance from the ground up, follow where my instincts in rehearsals lead me. We explore physical warm-ups, play improvisation games, and read scenes from my script. It is a lot of work, but I could not be happier.

After six weeks my play, *JOAN,* is presented by six actors playing multiple roles. A modern retelling of the story of Joan of Arc, *JOAN* is the story of a sullen teenager with three best friends who just happen to be saints.

Creating *JOAN* becomes a turning point in my life. The process is artistically completely satisfying. It is a singular experience that leads me to have more faith in myself as an artist. To follow the vision I have worked out in notebooks since my own college days and to write and stage a play with the physical presence of an ensemble of actors at the core, I realize I have evolved into a maker and shaper of my own brand of theatre.

With women winning Tonys and theatre companies adding plays by women to their former all-white-male seasons, I believe the revolution in theatre is about to begin. The Guerrilla Girls theatre committee prepares for the fight. We scratch our hairy heads for a fresh plan of attack.

I had access to contact numbers for producers, artistic directors, and more. A spy never reveals how they carry out their missions, so I cannot tell you how I had access to this information. I can only tell you that somehow these contacts were divided up and distributed among the Guerrilla Girls theatre committee members.

One Monday morning during Women's History Month (March), hundreds of theatre professionals receive, via fax, our "Oh! The Joys" poster accompanied by this cover letter:

> Greetings from the Guerrilla Girls! We have often been accused of being too negative. Therefore, in honor of Women's History Month, we have decided to create a poster that focuses on the bright side of being a woman in theatre. Enjoy!

We sign each fax with a big lipstick kiss and dub this "the Guerrilla Girls' theatre fax blitz."

Naming names made me giddy. There was nothing more satisfying than calling someone out on their track record of discrimination. From behind a mask and while using the name of a dead woman artist, it felt gutsy and profound. Who knew a fax machine could be a weapon in the war against sexism in theatre, utilized while sitting at my desk in a gravy-stained kimono, one hand holding a cup of coffee while the other presses and re-presses "send"?

Soon after our theatre fax blitz, Gertrude Stein picks up this message on our answering service:

> *You're shooting yourselves in the foot. Although I'm sympathetic, you should put faces on your mail. Some of what you say is off the mark and I resent it on one level. Get some feedback. Think about what you are saying before you send mail out without the opportunity to respond to it. Being anonymous is chicken. Let's have a meeting. I'm not going to defend myself, but this one-way communication is not a dialogue. You come off as a bunch of angry women, even though your cause is good.*

Our letterhead prominently features our phone number. This message, from the artistic director of a very successful not-for-profit theatre company, criticizes our use of masks and pseudonyms to spotlight our cause. He is correct in assuming we are a "bunch of angry women."

But wait, did he really say, "Let's have a meeting"? Gertrude confirms that yes, he said, "Let's have a meeting." We would love to have a meeting! I picture three or four gorilla-masked women, crammed into his office, discussing plays by women to include in his next season. We call him back and leave a message suggesting dates and times to meet. He does not return the call.

Important people in the theatre community begin to respond to me, but only when I have a gorilla mask jammed over my head. And only while wearing the mask do I summon up both the courage and the desire to point out the flaws of the system. It is a powerful perch and an easy position. I take no personal risk, duck the jabs critiquing my tactics as the pseudonymous masked avenger, Aphra Behn.

A gorilla-masked woman is easy to dismiss. Who cares if I, from behind a ridiculous mask, call you out on your sexist season? There is no heft in the arguments of me, a modern-day feminist Lone Ranger. I am not real. My methods are based in fable, my message an old parable, incomprehensible to many contemporary audiences.

While I initially rejoice at the few reactions to our fax blitz action, I realize that in many ways I am still being shoved aside.

Not ready to give in, the mask-wearing chicken known as Aphra Behn clucks and moves on.

While Aphra Behn is busy throwing brown bananas at Broadway marquees and pounding her chest at the announcement of another all-white-male season by a theatre company in New York City and beyond, I, the unmasked playwright/director, press on, writing, directing, and knocking on theatre doors. I am offered a position as the artistic director of a small theatre company in Scranton, Pennsylvania (where I produce five plays, three by women, all directed by women). One of my musicals is selected for Nagle Jackson's "Adapting for the Stage Workshop" at the Directors Company; I direct the work of a group of award-winning slam poets in the American Living Room series at the HERE Arts Center in SoHo. I read scripts and write coverage for the New York Theatre Workshop and direct a short play for a development series at New Georges.

Still, the theatre community feels smaller, much more insular and cliquish than it did when I first moved to New York. I continue to feel, at forty-four, that I am too old. No one is interested in producing *JOAN*. The rejection letters pile up. An undertone of skepticism lingers if I state I am a writer/director. My career feels stuck and stalled. I wait in the wings and suspect I have missed my cue.

The smell of the rubber is the only thing that calms my inner beast. With a gorilla mask securely over my head, Behn is the antidote to Kaz's sexism-in-theatre blues. Aphra Behn does not give a shit about skeptics or rejection letters. She knows that for every "no" to her, or any other woman playwright, there is a sticker in a toilet stall some-where that an innocent audience member is reading or a puzzled main-tenance worker is trying to scrape off.

Memorial Day Weekend, 1999. The Guerrilla Girls have been granted a weekend retreat at the Blue Mountain Center in the Adirondacks to regroup and relax. Twelve of us arrive on Friday night and settle in for forty-eight hours of productivity.

A schedule and agenda have been hammered out beforehand and everyone has had a chance to sign up to lead a brainstorming session. From mundane administrative issues to future goals, the weekend promises to strengthen our bonds as a collective with both work and play.

Since I joined the group we have not spent this much uninterrupted time together, and we use it well. I help to lead a discussion about how we might theatricalize our "Gigs" with focused audience participation, video, and the addition of new parody skits rooted in current events. Another Guerrilla Girl brings up terminology, how to succinctly talk about race and gender and the best choice of words for our posters. Occasionally we stray off topic and this results in some hilarious ideas: a Guerrilla Girls Cookbook, including recipes for Claude Cahun's Cross Dressing and Gertrude Stein's Cubist Jell-O Salad.

With a bright blue sky overhead on Sunday afternoon, we take our agenda outside to discuss our diversity. Claude Cahun makes an impassioned speech citing the work of men against sexism and how men would only enhance the Girls' mission. If we include male mem-bers, she adds, we will no longer be accused of what we fight against—discrimination as a women-only group.

— No.

— What?

— I don't want men in the group. The dynamics would completely change and I won't do it.

While Claude's argument is a good one, I am certain the safe meeting space of the Guerrilla Girls will dramatically change when males are allowed to be present, and I strongly voice my opposition. Other members favor adding men. I cannot bring myself to see their side. My fears confuse the group. I finally explain to everyone that I am a survivor of domestic violence and burst into tears. We vote to table the idea of adding men to another time.

Later, I am embarrassed, not because I am the only member to speak up against inviting men to join the Guerrilla Girls, but because I use my status as a survivor to justify my position. I still feel very guilty about my experience and as a result I rarely mention it. "I would never stay" is a common response to stories of domestic violence. I cringe when I hear sentences like, "I would get the hell out of there as soon as he laid one finger on me."

People know me as a strong activist and feminist. I do not talk about my past because I fear that when others hear it, they will understandably feel a little disappointed. They may judge me, believe that because so many years have passed there must be only one motivation for me to speak: I want my fifteen minutes of fame.

I am someone who has dedicated part of her life to fighting for women's voices to be heard. I open my own mouth and all I can feel is shame. The irony of these torments is not lost on me. For the first time, perhaps, I begin to think of what my commitment to silence has done for me all these years.

I think about it for a very long time.

I grab a pencil, open a small, spiral notebook, and poise the pencil over a blank page. I turn myself inside out and wonder what will happen when I tell my story? Are there advantages to breaking my silence?

What positive things might result if I let my story out, I write at the top of the page.

If I let my story out someone may read it. Young, old, married, single, mother, father, young adult, someone battered a long time ago or living in violence right now may read it. Someone who knows someone who knows someone else who is or has been beaten or raped or harassed on the street could read it. When they read it they will recognize their own story within mine. When they read it they are reminded that for many, violence is close by. Violence is personal. Peace begins inside a home.

Perhaps someone might, upon hearing my story, consider their own narrative and see it as very different from what they had previously believed. The personal journey of one could be a bridge to a discovery of a deep-seated truth in another.

If I let my story go others would release theirs as well.

Or not.

Perhaps my story will send the message that it is fine to keep your story right where it is, safely hidden away. It is okay to store your story, as I did, inside for as long as you wish. You can keep your story to yourself, wait on it, nurture it, remember it, and maybe someday let it go without a sound.

Or, you can let it out.

It took time and distance to embrace the essence of my narrative. When I accepted my own history, it felt as if I had been stung. My mouth went slack, my jaw came loose. I opened up my mouth and could no longer hold back. The words surged forward in waves.

As I consider the many rewards of telling my story, I turn the page of my spiral notebook to a fresh leaf of paper and write: What good will happen if I remain silent? Are there advantages to keeping my story inside? What is the benefit of never another word written?

I hold my pencil over the page.

I hold my pencil over the page.

Sunday, May 30, 1999. The moon is full and the night bright. The lake at Blue Mountain carries our voices across the mountains. After almost forty-eight hours of focusing on activism, someone suggests a midnight canoe trip. We yarr in unison and head for the boathouse. The croaking of frogs covers our laughter as we try to maneuver into the canoes with only the light of the moon to guide us.

"Hold on to the gunwales!" someone yells at Claude Cahun, who attempts to gracefully step into the stern of one of the canoes. "Hold on to the gunwales!" Claude has one foot in, then the other, then she is gone with a loud splash plop. Breaking the surface of the lake with a gasp, she cries, "What the hell is a gunwale?!"

Claude successfully climbs out of the lake into a canoe and slips to the back of a line of boats carrying unmasked feminist avengers quietly through the water. At one point we all put down our paddles and simply float along, the vivid round shape in the sky and the reflection it makes on the water our focus. We drift in complete silence for a full minute. We are women activists being carried gently into the twenty-first century.

11

1979, MALIBU

WE WIND OUR WAY FARTHER AND farther from the guts of the city of Los Angeles, cross the Malibu city line, and arrive at our bungalow where Bats waits for us.

The beach house is lined with dark wood wainscoting. An old-fashioned oval hooked rug covers a linoleum floor. There are two small bedrooms, a tiny kitchen, a bathroom, and a narrow living room with a fireplace and ocean-facing windows. Opposite the windows, a retro couch is parked under a bookshelf and a table with a cream-colored push-button phone on top occupies the center of the space. A deck wraps the house on two sides. A simple rope-and-pulley system lowers a wooden staircase, like a drawbridge, down to the sand below.

Our lives here are underscored by the constant, rhythmic whoosh of water crashing to the shore. The only certainty of our days and nights together, the waves will break and be sucked back into the sea.

⚡

The surf nudges me awake. Light filters through the slats in the shutters on the bedroom windows and I open my eyes to strange surroundings.

We fell asleep so very late, I recall, and a blush breaks across my heart. Not used to West Coast time, I shake the sweetness from my mind, carefully roll over, slowly stand, and make my way into the kitchen.

There is nothing but the inexhaustible ocean in front of me. I jump when Bill's arms reach around my waist from behind. He heralds our first perfect morning living together.

With two whole days off until shooting resumes, we throw on our bathing suits, grab the Frisbee, lower the stairs, and hit the sand. He throws Bats the Frisbee and she runs down the beach, stops to look back, and then jumps straight up to grip the airborne Frisbee between her teeth. She is tireless, and everyone on the beach stops to ask how she does it. Bill explains she is a natural. We take turns flipping the Frisbee through the air farther and farther. Not one throw evades Bats.

The waves are calm this morning. I wade into the water up to my thighs. Bill dives headfirst into the foam and swims straight out, stopping only to call out for me to join him. We head for the kelp line fifty feet from the shore. Bats swims with us until she is spooked and turns back to sit on the beach and keep watch.

The ocean is deep and dense; an underwater forest of bottle-green seaweed makes a natural barrier beyond the break of the waves. Bill grabs me in a float hold and grips me tight. Our legs beat beneath us as we mash our faces together and sink below the water. I break away from his arms, rise up to catch a breath just as he takes off, a windmill of arms taunting me in a race back to shore. He beats me to the sand, grabs the Frisbee, and runs back to the bungalow. Bats receives a rinse with the outdoor hose and then Bill aims the water on my shoulders and lets the cold stream help his fingers peel the bathing suit from my skin.

⚡

In the afternoon we drive up into the Malibu Canyon where Bill's costar, Blair Brown, lives with her partner, Richard Jordan. Their house is a funky old haven down a dirt ravine, surrounded by eucalyptus trees and rocky canyon walls. Funny and full of love, Blair and Richard become our perfect best friends and we spend almost every weekend together. Richard and Bill throw darts on the terrace or sit down to a focused game of chess while Blair and I make trips to the Malibu Country Mart to pick up fresh flowers and food. In the evening hours, as the sun slips behind the mountains, we nibble on Blair's savory meals, sip red wine, and debate around the table. If the night turns cold, we head inside, where Richard lights a fire and pulls out a book. He reads a Shakespearean sonnet or a poem by Keats with great emotion, then hands the book to Bill, who reciprocates with a brilliant interpretation of his own. A great tension is released on these Saturdays. With no work tomorrow, everyone forgets that Monday, and the demands of a making a film like *Altered States,* will eventually come.

The moment Bill and Richard's discussions turn into incoherent arguments, Blair and I signal to each other that it is time for us to break up the party and for Bill and me to make our escape back to the beach. The drive home is pitch-black and treacherous.

⚡

The Monday after I arrive Bill goes back to work. A driver picks him up very early in the morning. Just before he leaves, at 5 a.m., he gently wakes me and reminds me of the map and directions he has left on the table. He will call me to let me know what time I should drive to the studio to meet him.

Altered States is filmed at the Burbank Studios. It is an easy drive down the Pacific Coast Highway and up through Malibu Canyon Road to the Ventura Freeway. I pull up to the studio security booth, roll down my window, and give my name to the guard, who checks me off a list and waves me through.

Going ten miles per hour, I pass grips carrying cables and extras walking by in alien costumes. Golf carts buzz by carrying important-looking people to their destinations. I am in the middle of a world I have only seen on television. It is just like the movies, only it *is* the movies.

I have to adjust my eyes when I enter the *Altered States* soundstage. I ask the first person I see if they know where I might find Bill. I am led around a path lined with neatly organized equipment and told to wait in a director's chair with Bill's name on it. In the distance I hear something going on but I cannot see it. I do my best imitation of a statue until I hear a buzzer go off and there is Bill bounding around the corner, smiling, a handful of people behind him. He introduces me to some of the crew, who all tell me how much Bill talks about me.

After the day wraps we go across the street to the Smoke House with some of the crew to drink and eat dinners of rare ribeye steaks with baked potatoes smothered in butter and sour cream.

The next day is the same. And the next day and the next. My mornings begin to blend together. After two weeks I decide I have to do something else with my time.

Bill speaks fluent French. If we are going to Paris maybe I should take French classes. I pull out the phone book and call around to a bunch of language schools until I find a month-long intensive course for two thousand bucks. Bill thinks it is too expensive.

I find a modern dance class in Santa Monica and drive there a few times a week. It feels good to move and is a fine (and inexpensive) class, but I need something more.

When Bill asked me to come to LA and live with him, he promised I would not have to worry about money. The details of exactly what this meant are never worked out. He is very generous except when he is not. Various amounts of cash are left out for me on the table to pay for food and gas. I stash the bills in my purse and dole them out for our necessities. Sometimes he asks me if I need more money, other times I have to remind him I am down to my last five bucks. At first we act casual about this arrangement. Eventually, I think he either resents it or fears the gesture of leaving money for me on the table with a cream-colored push-button phone on top means more than what it is—some kind of symbol he will take care of me for the rest of my life. I am not looking to be taken care of. We have problems. Our physical rows were not left behind in New York City. They followed us to Malibu and increase in intensity a little each time. As soon as they pass, I accept his apologies and his promises to stop. I do not realize I will start to cycle through to that promise as regularly as the tide.

And then there is the status of his divorce, which I falsely believe has been finalized and merely awaits the signing of some papers. As for marriage, he pronounces we do not need it. We are more married than married people, heart to heart and soul to soul.

But what am I going to do with my life here in Malibu? There are very few theatre productions in LA to audition for. One night we have dinner with the *Altered States* production designer, Richard MacDonald, and his wife, the costume designer Ruth Myers, who turns to me and says,

— We have to get you a job! I know what it's like being "the girlfriend."

I am very grateful someone has voiced what I secretly feel. Sadly, I never see Ruth again to ask her what kind of a job she thinks I could get.

↯

It is the middle of the night. We scream at each other. He threatens to kill himself. A carving knife in one hand, he stands over the sink, presses the tip of the blade into a blue vein in his wrist and warns me he will shove it up and into his forearm at any moment. I cry and plead with him to please stop. His face is an erupting volcano of pain and ferocity. Something implodes inside of him and he cannot stop. He pulls the knife away from his hand and brandishes it in my face, now declares he is going to kill me too.

The ocean picks up our voices and they echo across the Pacific Coast Highway, bounce back out to sea, travel up and into outer space.

Bill presses the knife once again against his wrist. Then, *bang, bang, bang!* Someone is at the back gate.

The sound freezes us in our spots and we lock eyes. *Who the hell would that be at this hour?* we silently convey to each other with open mouths. The interruption jolts us out of our private nightmare and threatens to expose it.

— Hello? Are you in trouble? Do you need help?

Someone calls to us from over the back gate.

— We were driving by and we heard someone screaming. Can we help you?

Is this person kidding? They were driving by on the highway and heard us?

With the knife still in his hand Bill runs to the back gate. He swings it open to reveal a young man and young woman, both dressed in jean jackets and sneakers. They look like hippies.

— Sorry, but we heard shouting. It sounded like someone needed help.

Good call.

I hover behind Bill, not sure of my part. I notice his grip on the knife is loose. It now dangles from his hand as if he was in the middle of making dinner.

— It sounded like something bad might be happening so we stopped and knocked to see if we can help.

Bill swings the back gate open wide and steps to one side.

— Would you like to come in?

Bill hustles the couple inside and gestures for them to sit on the sofa. They both squat down and hover on the edge of the couch.

— Jesus loves you.

— Excuse me?

Bill has drawn a chair up and sits opposite the couple. I remain standing and wonder if maybe I should offer them something.

— Do you know that Jesus loves you? He wants you to love each other.

The woman takes the knife out of Bill's hands and holds it out to me. I reach for it and robotically move to the kitchen where I hide it under the sink.

— No need to do anything but love each other, I hear her say.

I step back inside the living room, and noiselessly float to one side of our unexpected guests.

— May we pray with you?

Bill looks up at me. A few minutes ago we were in the depths of hell. Now a strange couple is in our midst and they want to pray. The woman stands and holds out her hand toward Bill and the other toward me. Instinctively, I reach out and grasp her hand. Bill stands and does the same. The man takes hold of my other hand and reaches out with his other arm toward Bill. No one says a word. The four of us, who just seconds ago were strangers, now stand hand in hand. Across the circle, Bill and I look at each other. Finally the man closes his eyes and speaks.

— Heavenly Father, please look down on this couple and let them feel the love they have for each other in their hearts. Let them feel the love you have for them, Father, and I ask that you bless them and take all thoughts from their minds except thoughts of love.

I am dreaming this.

— Protect this couple, and watch over them. Keep them from harming each other. May they always feel your love and the love they have for each other. Amen.

My palm is sweaty and cold. The woman squeezes it before dropping it as abruptly as she grasped it.

— We'll leave you our phone number. Just in case.

The man scribbles something on a piece of paper on the table and, like a dream that shreds itself into nothing before waking, just as quickly as they arrived they are gone.

As soon as Bill closes the back gate he turns to me in silence. We go back to the living room, sit on the couch, turn to face each other, and both burst out laughing. We laugh so hard we fall on the floor. For five-plus minutes we laugh until our guts ache.

— What the fuck was that all about? Jesus loves us?

— You could not write a more bizarre scene if you tried!

Someone heard us. Our secret is out. Someone heard us in our isolated bungalow on the beach in the middle of one of our worst moments. Someone heard me.

Once our laughter subsides these are my thoughts. For the first time there has been a witness to the violence.

Exhausted, we go into the bedroom, lie down, and spoon each other before falling into a deep and sound sleep.

The next day I find the piece of paper with the phone number on it and throw it away.

$$\lightning$$

The summer comes and the days drone on. Every day is sunny and warm. Our house is next to a set of public access stairs to the beach and the crowds come, some to spread out their beach towels right under our deck for a bit of shade. A few times a beachgoer will yell up to me, ask if they can use my phone or the toilet. I let no one in. Bats is my great protector, barks loudly if anyone makes an attempt to climb our steps.

I begin to fill my days by smoking a lot of pot. At the table in front of the windows I sit, lit up and blitzed-out, a half-baked to-do list in front of me. I will build a wall under our deck so no one can put their blanket down there. Maybe I will order a sign that says, *Keep Out! Private Property!* and nail it to the outside of the deck. Even better, I will build a fence down to the tide line to keep people from parking their beach chairs directly in front of my view. And until I can get all these projects together I will turn on the outside water, uncoil the hose, and spend an hour watering the plants on the deck, spraying and spraying and spraying until the sand below is uninvitingly soaked through.

$$\lightning$$

One day I stare just a bit too long at the ocean and it dawns on me. What I should do has been right in front of me all along.

At Camp Blue Bay I was a lifeguard and taught swimming and

boating, but my classes had to be signed off by the head of waterfront, an official Red Cross water safety instructor. With a little bit of research I find out an American Red Cross water safety instructor course will be offered at a high school nearby. It meets on Tuesday afternoons for six weeks. Perfect! I will qualify as a Red Cross water safety instructor and get a job teaching swimming.

The Agoura High School pool, where the class takes place, is a thirty-minute drive from the bungalow up Kanan Dume Road. The other students are blonde young girls and tanned surfer guys, carefree California teenagers, four or five years younger than me and recent graduates of Agoura High. I am much closer in experience and maturity to my classmates. As a student in the class, I return to my world, a world without pressure.

The teacher is a male athletic coach at the high school, and I am surprised at how nice he is to me and how hard he tries to make me feel comfortable. Everyone in class still lives with their parents and are about to go off to college, some for the first time. When they ask me what I do I simply say I just moved here from New York with my boyfriend and nothing more. After class we all go our separate ways; often the others will head off to eat pizza together or go to the beach. They never ask me to join them, but secretly I wish they would. This class is the only thing I have in LA that is completely mine, and I treasure it.

On the day we learn CPR, the instructor pairs us off and tells us we will practice on each other. I am partnered with one of the surfer guys, and as he lies down in front of me and I place my hands on his face, tilt his head back, and put my mouth over his, all I can think about is how jealous Bill would be if he saw me do this. The power in making a choice, one that Bill would not like, feels pleasurable. Bill often accuses me of flirting with other men, but I never have. I do not want anyone else. I savor this moment, however, stretch it out a tad longer than I should, blow twice into the lungs of my partner. The minute I pull back and look down I realize there is nothing sexual about performing CPR on a young man in board shorts. My thoughts embarrass me.

↯

— I don't want you at the studio tomorrow. I will have one of the drivers give me a ride home.

Bill is lying on the couch reading a book. He does not look up.

— Why?

— I just don't want you there!

— But what am I supposed to do instead?

— Whatever you want!

— I pick you up every day.

— Stupid. Dumb and stupid. You are a clunk, you know that?

As quietly as possible, I slip into the bathroom, shut the door, and step into the shower. The conversation leads to a familiar and unsafe place. Time and space between us is the only chance I have to take the charge out of the atmosphere. It is early Sunday, sunny and warm again. No reason it should not be the start of a beautiful day.

I finish my shower and stand on the bath mat to towel off. The bathroom door flies open so hard that it slams with a whack against the wall and then *wah-wah* vibrates, like an electric guitar. Suddenly, the place I stand falls out below me and I fly up and into the air. Just like the tablecloth trick, where a magician attempts to pull a tablecloth out from a table set with dishes and silverware and wine goblets without moving anything except the tablecloth is what this feels like, except I am a wine goblet and the bath mat is the tablecloth and the trick has failed. I am about to come crashing to the ground and shatter into a million pieces. My hand hits the floor first, then my arm, shoulder, and finally my body makes contact with a *thunk*. Motion, noise I do not recognize, and then I am dragged naked across the floor. I use my feet to stop myself in the doorjamb but cannot hold on for long. Screams, shouts, slaps, a pillow comes down over my face and just when I think I will pass out it is taken away. My eyes close tight. Hands move in front of my face. My head slams down and I see a flash, like a camera going off, and then blackness. It repeats, white flash into black, white flash into black. A voice screams into my ear, his shouts are so close I feel spit hit my cheek. How long will this go on? Can I make it stop? As soon as I can get away I will. I will leave this place. I will leave this place forever and never come back. Bats is a mound of fur in the corner and I imitate her, scrunch my head into my body, make myself as small an object as possible. I am a shut suitcase. I am an empty TV box. I am a sleeping dog. Inanimate and dead, I wait for it to be over.

Ten minutes, or maybe it is hours later, I come back around to the plash of water. Look at the pathetic girl I have become.

My finger hurts. I crawl around the room, whimper like a broken Betsy Wetsy doll, in search of clothes, anything to put on. I must get away. He calls out to me. I do not respond. I want to find the car keys before it is too late. I need help. My finger does not look right.

— Get away from me. Don't touch me. I'm leaving and I'm never coming back.

He stands away from me with one hand out.

— Let me help you.

We play the scene, as good as one on the National Geographic Channel: man tames wild, wounded beast with a slow approach, shows his kindness, gains her trust little by little. He will not hurt her anymore.

He puts me in the car and takes me to the Malibu emergency room. A technician X-rays my finger and tells me it is broken.

— How did you do this? a doctor asks.

— Falling, I say. I fell.

It is not a lie. I really did fall. Just like a wine goblet tossed into the air.

A nurse puts a splint on my finger and tapes it up. Bill pays and they send us home. That night I sleep in the next room. Monday morning I grab the car keys first thing. I will get away. I will go somewhere.

I throw some stuff into my hand bag and step onto the deck. Tiny squares of note paper are taped all across the fence, a dozen of them line the way to the back gate. They are words of love and remorse and perpetual regret.

The notes will be followed by an expensive gift. When that happens I know it is over. It will never happen again because it is the very worst it ever got and we cannot go there again and survive. So I stay.

$$\lightning$$

July 5, 1979: I stare at the ceiling, call back memories of our first date and the production of *Fifth of July,* by Lanford Wilson, at Circle Rep.

— Okay, but don't come in me.

We are in the bedroom. I did not have time to put in my diaphragm. Bill shifts on top of me, my hands grip his body.

— Did you hear what I just said? I said don't come in me. Bill? Don't come in me, don't . . . did you just . . . !?"

Shit! SHIT! I feel his sperm release inside of me and head up my cervix, swim forward through my fallopian tube and take direct aim. In twenty minutes one of those sperm will slam up against my egg with a focused force and I will be fertilized. My gut, my instinct, my sixth sense tells me, I am pregnant.

Over-the-counter pregnancy tests are brand-new. Two weeks later I pick one up at the drugstore. It is positive.

Bill is happy. He is lighter. He is loving and more relaxed. I am happy he is happy. But I am not happy. I am twenty-four years old. I do not want to have a baby.

I do not want to have a baby and I know I will not change my mind. There is no way I will bring another human being into our mad world. We have so much to work on. After we sort it all out I will think about having his child. For now I do not want to have a baby.

He will never marry me and has told me this more than once. We do not need to be married. Not that it would affect my decision if he proposed. Even if he got down on one knee and said . . .

— Will you, stupid, worthless, piece-of-shit, garbage, whore clunk, marry me?

I would reply . . .

— Abso-fucking-lutely not, asshole.

Even if he said . . .

— I love you and no one else but you and I want to be with you for the rest of my life, please marry me and have my baby.

No, not even then. No, no, no. I do not want to have a baby.

Having his baby will not fix our relationship. I cannot bring a child into my messed-up and often sick, dependent, remediless, angry life. I do not want to have a baby.

The morning of my abortion Bill drives me to the doctor and insists on being with me during the procedure. The doctor agrees to meet us in his office beforehand instead. He asks if we have questions and Bill wants to know if I am going to be okay. He wants only reassurance I will be all right.

I am given an anesthetic but remain awake. The procedure is straightforward and routine except at the end I suddenly feel very nauseated. The doctor asks me what kind of blood I have. As soon as I reply my blood is A-negative, everyone flies out of the room. I find out later that women with A-negative blood will have complications if their fetus's blood is Rh-positive. If even a small amount of Rh-negative blood comes into contact with Rh-positive blood, antibodies form and attack. The doctor rushes back in to give me some kind of shot to stop the process and about thirty minutes after I get the injection I am free to leave.

On the drive home Bill stops at the McDonald's on the Pacific Coast Highway. I nurse a container of milk while he finishes his burger. Glad it is over, I sleep for the entire weekend. On Monday I decide to go for a run but do not get far before feeling sick. When I tell Blair about this she yells at me and makes me promise to not try to exercise again.

I really just want to forget all about it, and that is what I do until my parents get their insurance statement. Since I am still on their insurance plan they ask me if I had an abortion. When I tell them yes, they want to know if I am all right. From the abortion I am fine, I think. Yes, I say to them. Yes, I am all right.

$$\lightning$$

The radio alarm, tuned to KCRW, snaps on with the morning's news: *Today is an even-number day for gas rationing. If the last digit on your license plate is even you can head for the pumps and buy gas today and only—*

Bill slams the radio off and drags himself into the shower. Outside the bedroom window I hear car tires crunch on the gravel and stop. Bill's driver is here. The car door opens, followed by a light knock on the back gate. Bill opens the outside bathroom door and yells over the gate he will be right out.

Bill treads back into the bedroom and steps into his pants. The hum of his zipper, the chink of his belt buckle, the click of his plastic-tipped shoelaces on the floor float through the air. He stuffs something into his briefcase, his script. The snap of a lighter and an inhale. His first Winston of the day. Suddenly his lips are inches from my face. As he kneels down beside me I feel his fine, damp hair tickle my forehead, his smooth lips kiss mine. "Call me later," he murmurs.

The gate bangs, a car door slams, the gravel crunches again as the car drives away. It is still pitch-black out. I turn over onto my side and pull a blanket over my shoulder. Bats snuggles up next to me. The sound of the surf floods my ears. I count the seconds between each rolling wave—one, two, three, crash; one, two, three, crash—and finally drift back to sleep.

At eight o'clock my eyes open. I get up and straighten the blanket over the mattress. Beyond the living room windows the blue Pacific Ocean rumbles easily to the shore in short, frothy waves. Pelicans sweep by, pause, and dive-bomb for fish. I look for whale spouts in the distance but do not see any today. What will I do this morning?

Throwing on a pair of shorts and an old T-shirt, I go out on the deck and lower the stairs to the sand. I pick up the Frisbee and head down the beach, Bats nips at the Frisbee and bolts ahead, anxious for me to throw it to her. I throw high, low, right, left, into the waves. She retrieves them all. Sometimes it looks as if she can jump fourteen feet straight up in the air.

After our walk we have breakfast. I might read a book or write in my journal or work on my theatre piece about my experiences waiting tables at Jimmy Day's. Maybe new ideas for songs, dances, and dialogue will spew from my pen. Perhaps in the hours before I have to leave to pick up Bill at the studio, I will work out scenes and imagine I am a future female Richard Schechner, and one day will lead an experimental workshop production of my play. Or maybe I will just light up a joint and do the laundry.

Around ten I call Bill's trailer. If he is there I ask him if he knows what time he will be done for the day. Sometimes he tells me to call back later. Sometimes he tells me he does not know, just come at four. Sometimes he tells me he needs something and I should come earlier and bring him what he needs. Today he tells me to be there at four.

At three o'clock I lock Bats inside the house and drive to the studio in the rented red Mustang. I swerve along Malibu Canyon Road, wind right and left and right and left through the bare brown and green canyons to Las Virgenes Road to the 101 to Burbank Studios. I pull into the big front gate and the guard waves me through with a smile. I park in Bill's spot right next to the soundstage and head for his trailer. If he is not in his trailer it means he is in makeup or in costume or shooting on the soundstage. I head to the soundstage, find the canvas chair with his name on it, sit down and wait.

A member of the costume crew walks by.

— Where were you today? she asks as if I was invited to the set and did not show up. He really needed you today, she states.

She tells me they shot difficult dream sequences and flashbacks and Bill had to be in his horrible latex bodysuit the whole time. Now I feel terrible. Bill said nothing about this.

The assistant director brings me word; Bill is wrapped for the day and will be in his trailer as soon as he is out of costume. I go back to the trailer and wait for him. The second he opens the trailer doors and climbs in I can see he is completely wiped out.

This is the point where I want to put him in the car and drive him home and cook him a chicken dinner and put him to bed. This is the point where I want to insist we go back to the beach, the healing beach, the tranquil beach immediately. This is where my instincts ignite and I want to grab him by the hand and drag him to the car like a child and if he does not come to scold and humiliate him until he obeys me. I do not do any of those things because this is the point where I feel inadequate. This is the point where I feel guilty for getting up late and writing in my journal and smoking a joint and looking fresh as a daisy. This is the point where the fact that I am here in Los Angeles with absolutely no demands on me, absolutely not one single responsibility except to drive a rented car to the studio and back every day, makes me the enemy.

I open my arms for Bill to fall into. I cannot imagine the physical demands, the mental needs, the emotional mandates acting in a feature film impose. I cannot fathom why someone who is on the precipice of stardom would feel insecure, worthless, and lonely. If I knew better I would see what a mismatched pair we are and how incapable we both have become of seeing what the other is going through.

There is day and there is night. There is dusk and dawn, but we do not know the subtle differences. We are only one thing or the other. At this moment, at five or six o'clock, we are morphing into something blue and ominous. A chasm, much like the void in *Altered States* the genetically transformed Dr. Eddie Jessup falls through, is about to open up and engorge us.

What we do next is up to him. I wait for him to tell me. We are going out to dinner with so-and-so or with so-and-so. In the trailer, he pours us drinks and changes his clothes. He says goodbye to every-body as we head for the car.

— Good work today, Bill.

— Thank you. Not so good, but thanks.

I bet it was good. I bet it was great. Why does he doubt his own talent?

We reach the car, he takes the keys and gets behind the wheel. Bill drives us out of the lot and we head for some expensive restaurant or some dive bar full of people I do not know and he is on to the next phase of his day where he will talk and drink and talk and drink and drink and talk longer and louder than anyone at the table.

I will sit near people I just met and try to find a common ground with someone. Before I can formulate a sentence that I believe sounds fairly intelligent, Bill has already lifted off and reached cruising altitude, vocally conceptualizing the art of acting or the genre of moviemaking with sentences full of long words and limited punctuation. Now no one is interested in me, or in anyone else at the table for that matter, as all eyes are on the luminous orator and his ability to make you grapple with exactly what he is saying for a nanosecond or two before you get completely lost on the river of verbosity. It is too late for anyone at the table, we have all walked up the ramp and boarded the Bill-Boat; a mental excursion of wonder we shall travel upon whether we like it or not. With Bill as our captain we motor forward, occasionally reaching out for a phrase or a word we might recognize to keep us from sliding completely adrift and into the ocean of incomprehensibility.

Shut up! Stop trying to impress us with words and heady ideas already. Just be yourself, ya big, handsome lug!

I want to say those words to Bill but never do. For a second he may pause to briefly interject some praise for me, his loving girlfriend, or, more likely, a quick flagdown of the waitress and an order of another round smack in the middle of a spontaneous sitting essay on some-thing obscure like divination and/or death.

I know what will happen next. Everyone at the table will fall in love in five, four, three, two, one, bingo—down, down the waterfall we tumble with Bill because he makes us feel like not only are we smart enough to follow his velocious train of thought, but we are also the only people in the universe who truly get him.

I watch this show every night. Bill invokes a spell so charismatic, it needs no warranty. On the one or two occasions I witness someone not willing to get caught up in his words I am genuinely impressed. Strong and rare are those who resist him, especially women. It is with difficulty that most refuse to go along on a trip through Bill's fathomless it-is-the-journey-not-the-destination mind.

We are always the last ones to leave the place because he has to have the last drink, the last line, the last thought, the last word. Bill has to pick up the bill because Bill can afford it and Bill has commanded the attention of all of us for hours and did they not listen and nod yes, yes, yes to him in fantastic agreement all evening? Maybe if Bill buys them dinner and drinks they will forgive him his brief spell of insanity and see him for who he really is, a lonely man adrift in the world with the same wants all of us have: to be accepted as a human being, to not be put on a pedestal and praised just because you are gorgeous, talented, brilliant, and brave; to be loved and understood. Just a little love and understanding, please. Love me. Love me. Love. Me.

Drawing the curtains of the night closed, all that is left is for us to get home to the beach. Even though we are both drunk or high or drunk and high he drives us there. I sit in the passenger seat and all is silent for a bit and then we get into it.

HIM: Why didn't I speak and what did I think and why was I flirting with this one or why was that one looking at me and I saw him stroke your arm.

HER: Why were you looking at her and did you sleep with her before I got here?

HIM: Do not ask questions, it is none of your business.

By some miracle we get home in one piece and enter the house and Bats has peed on the rug and ripped up the newspaper. Bill will yell at

Bats, she will shrink and cower and look to me, but he knows what to do to mold her into an obedient dog. He will tie her up in the garage on a very short line. This is how it is done, he explains. This is how to train a dog. The line looks too short but I say nothing. I should take her off the line but I say nothing. I should rescue her but I do nothing even though Bats looks at me with her sad brown eyes as if to say, *You know this is not right.*

I cannot make it stop for myself, how shall I make it stop for you, I say to Bats silently in my head. The things I might have ended if I did more than shut down my own guilt. I am worthless.

After Bill puts Bats in the garage he will come back into the house, grab me by my hair, and slam my head into the wall. I will fall back to the floor and then he will be on top of me, his huge lanky frame will cover me, his enormous hands shall slap the top of my head as I try to block the blows with my arms, which causes his anger to detonate and pin both of my wrists to the floor. His fingers will circle my wrists and squeeze so tight I cannot break free. As I squirm, I will feel my wrists get hot and sweaty and the blood vessels underneath my skin burst and squish. Suddenly he will be off me. I will flip over to my knees as he stands up and kicks me in the side and I crawl toward the bathroom because it is the only place I can lock myself in. Sometimes I will get there and sometimes I will not and sometimes it ends after five minutes and sometimes it ends after thirty minutes and sometimes it feels like it ends after two hours and sometimes it feels like it never ends. Where is he now? He is nowhere to be seen so I go into the second bedroom and I close the door and I try to fall asleep and I do and then I feel wet on my face and I open my eyes and he is over me, tears drip from his blue eyes as he states he is sorry and asks can I ever forgive him and will I stay with him if he promises never to do it again. And I say yes, of course I will stay with him, because I love him deeply. Endless is my love for him like blood, like power, like sharpness, like he is me and I am him and we are connected and we are the only ones for each other, the only ones who understand each other. Now the ocean is no longer calm: it rages and it pounds on the shore and it pounds and pounds and pounds as he takes me by the hand and leads me back to our bed where we will make love over and over and over until the radio alarm, tuned to KCRW, snaps on with the morning's news and it starts all over again.

12

2000–2001,
NEW YORK CITY

I SCHEDULE *JOAN,* REWRITTEN AND REWORKED, for the Northeast Theatre Ensemble's 1999–2000 season, where I am in my first year as artistic director. This production, which I also direct, is even more successful than the last. The audience responds with gusto, the critics rave, the actors and designers have their own satisfying artistic experiences. The TNT production of *JOAN* is honored as one of the best productions of the year by the *Scranton Times.*

JOAN would not have gotten this far if it had not been endorsed by me. No outsider read my play and chose to produce it. I was hired as a producer and picked my own play. Even though the production was very successful, I wonder if I might feel better about it if I had not been the advocate of my own work.

My goals have always been to put out the best work possible. So where does this feeling I have failed come from? At the back of my brain is a constant desire to be validated by others. Standing ovations, rave reviews, and awards are not as satisfying for a play I practically self-produced. Something in me cannot stop longing for someone else to take over and say my work is good. I want to pass over the reins to others who then bring my theatrical ideas to fruition. I want someone else to produce my play. Because only when someone else puts the energy and the funding of their theatre behind me will I consider myself to be a success. I pine to be accepted as a member of the established, patriarchal theatre community.

Just as I make it a goal to get a paid acting job to consider myself an actor, as a playwright I can only legitimize myself as a playwright when someone else picks my play out of the pile and says, *We want to put our money behind this*. From the moment I declare myself an artist I am asked, over and over, the same questions: "Where might I have seen your work?" "What have you written I might have seen staged?" "What have you been in?" No wonder I believe I am only an artist if someone else has taken a chance on me—hired me, produced me, paid me to be allowed to stand up and declare, *I am an artist*.

I admit I give away the power of my artistic self that way. The belief in my work and my abilities should not rest outside of me and be beyond my control. If I have to remind myself over and over to stop worrying about who is going to like the stuff I make up, it just makes it all the more difficult to settle down and create it. *Relax and make art,* I want to tell myself.

I tie my own artistic hands together when I harbor a dream of making it, plays produced across the globe, my name in lights on Broadway. I have worked steadily at creating theatre almost since the time I graduated college and moved to New York. I have produced plays across the globe with Guerrilla Girls On Tour! Where did this idea come from that I cannot completely let go of: I am not yet a successful artist. Do I harbor a secret desire to be famous?

I have to believe that a part of the reason I continue to work as a Guerrilla Girl is out of frustration with my nonstatus in the male-dominated ranks of the theatre community. Even though Aphra Behn infiltrates those ranks, I wonder if I spend too much time on my work as a Guerrilla Girl and not enough time on my own art. If Aphra gets noticed, is that not enough? My activist work and my artistic output begin to blend, as do my two identities.

The arts are often held up as the last bastion of liberalism. A quick survey of theatre being produced in the tri-state area in 2000 uncovers this: the bigger the theatre, the less diverse and inclusive its mainstage season. Producers and artistic directors often excuse the "whiteness" of their main offerings with "staged-reading series" of plays by women and/or artists of color in their smaller spaces on off nights.

Thus, audiences are used to seeing just one kind of play. To introduce them to the works of women and artists of color, who just might present a different kind of theatrical experience than a white male might, is a risk no one seems to want to take. To assume your audience is not curious or hungry enough for new work is a mistake.

Q: How does the theatre change?

A: Very slowly. And only when every playwright, actor, director, choreographer, producer, designer, theatre owner, artistic director, and audience member stands up and dictates a new vision of an inclusive theatre by refusing to continue the status quo.

We want to get everyone involved in our mission to quash discrimination in the theatre. Maybe we can enlist the help of Broadway theatregoers to sticker Broadway bathroom toilet stalls.

In the heart of Times Square is the TKTS booth, a popular place offering discounted tickets to Broadway and off-Broadway shows. During a Wednesday matinee, Lorraine Hansberry, Hallie Flanagan, and I don our gorilla masks and descend on the Times Square TKTS booth, armed with 8.5-by-11-inch stickers of our

"Oh! The Joys of Being a Woman Playwright" poster along with a
note that reads:

> *Today we are asking you to help us change American theatre by going to the*
> *toilet. When you go to the theatre put up this sticker in the bathroom and help*
> *us flush out discrimination in New York theatres.*
>
> *Thank you for being a Guerrilla Girl (or Baboon Boy) for a day!*

The line is long at the TKTS booth. We anticipate that a major collaboration with the Broadway audience is about to occur. As we walk
up and down the line, we meet many eager to accept our handouts
and directives. Unfortunately, most of them think we are cast members
from *The Lion King*.

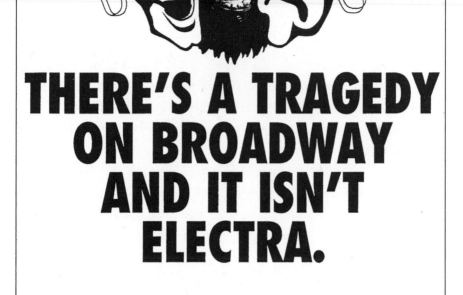

THERE'S A TRAGEDY ON BROADWAY AND IT ISN'T ELECTRA.

Only 8% of the plays and less than 1% of the musicals on Broadway were written by women.* Guerrilla Girls think that's even sadder than a Greek tragedy. There's only one explanation for what's currently playing:

DISCRIMINATION.

*Play: *Art.* Musicals: one-half of the book of *The Lion King;* one-fifth of the book of *It Ain't Nothin' But the Blues;* one-third of *Ragtime* (lyrics).

A PUBLIC SERVICE MESSAGE FROM **GUERRILLA GIRLS** CONSCIENCE OF THE THEATRE WORLD
5 3 2   L a G U A R D I A   P L A C E ,   # 2 3 7 •   N Y, N Y   1 0 0 1 2
f E m a i l :   g g @ g u e r r i l l a g i r l s . c o m

The Guerrilla Girls are an absurdist group, you have to understand. We know we're not going to change the world. We have to do something or we'll go nuts. You go on. What can you do? You just go on.[17]

IT IS TIME FOR THE GUERRILLA GIRLS TO ORGANIZE A PROTEST OF THE TONY AWARDS!

Who would not want to be a Guerrilla Girl for a day and fight sexism on Broadway? We invite everyone we know to protest the Tony Awards and imagine our Tony action will be a huge gathering of people wearing gorilla masks.

The early days of the Internet and the invention of e-mail connect us to more allies than we have ever had access to before (social networking is not yet a trend). We send out a call, request our e-mail be forwarded widely, imagine hundreds of people responding to our invitation: meet us on the steps of Saint Patrick's Cathedral on June 4, 2000, where we will march to Radio City Music Hall to protest the fifty-fourth annual Tony Awards.

The full-headed gorilla masks we wear are protest-prohibitive. We cannot effectively voice our dissent inside a wall of rubber. It we want to pull off a successful protest we have to come up with a way to be LOUD!

Enter the Art Cheerleaders, Boston art-school students dedicated to heightening the connection between the arts and community interests through cheerleading.

IT'S ART! IT'S ART!
SO GET DOWN ON YOUR KNEES

---

17 Gertrude Stein, *Theatre* magazine, 1999.

CAUSE WE'RE THE MIGHTY ARTISTS
AND WE DO AS WE PLEASE
IT'S ART! IT'S ART!
NOT THAT SHIT ON TV
CAUSE WE'RE THE MIGHTY ARTISTS
AND WE DO AS WE PLEASE[18]

Gertrude Stein has the idea to ask the Art Cheerleaders to collaborate with us and become our voices. They jump in and take over planning the vocal part of our protest, with new cheers specifically for the Tony Awards:

A TONY IS BALONEY
CUZ THE SYSTEM DOESN'T PLACE
VALUE ON THE WORK OF WOMEN
AND THAT'S A DISGRACE![19]

We print our "There's a Tragedy on Broadway . . ." poster on the back of black silk capes, a factitious move to blend us in with award attendees and other red-carpet looks. Two weeks before the Tonys, we send out our e-mail missive:

CALLING ALL GIRLS! Come be an honorary Guerrilla Girl for a day! The Guerrilla Girls will put a spotlight on racism and sexism on Broadway on June 4, 2000, at the Fifty-Fourth Annual Tony Awards. In our second appearance outside the awards, we will sing, chant, and give out our latest poster making fun of the long history of discrimination in the theatre world. We invite any and all women, children, and men who would like to fight

---

18 Written by the original 1997 School of the Museum of Fine Arts (SMFA) Cheerleaders; used by permission.

19 Written by the second iteration of the Art Cheerleaders in 2000; used by permission.

discrimination in theatre to join us and be Guerrillas for a day. Meet on the steps of Saint Patrick's Cathedral, Fifth Avenue between Fiftieth and Fifty-First, on June 4 at 4:15 p.m. We'll distribute "masks" and copies of our latest poster to anyone who shows up, then march on to Radio City Music Hall (Fifty-First and Sixth) to greet the Tony Award nominees.

VOICE-OVER: *While I support your endeavor to highlight injustices in the system, I have to wonder: Why do you care so much? What's the point of looking for approval from such a ridiculous old gaggle of has-beens as the American Theatre Wing? Why not put your energy into the creation of an art they cannot deny or belittle you for? While it's fun to complain, especially in costume, it does very little for our real cause in the long run, which is the reshaping of power systems patriarchal and racist, especially in the arts. Why nag them? Make your own awards!*

This person, who responded to the e-mail call, has a point. Why not work to create an alternative to Broadway? Maybe we will think about this later. Right now we have a protest to organize!

To the editor of the New York Times. *For the second time, we have chosen the annual Tony Awards as a perfect opportunity to point to and make fun of the seemingly endless trends of racism and sexism in American theatre. Since 1947 more than 100 Tonys have gone to Broadway directors. Only one has gone to a woman for directing a play and one to a woman for directing a musical. Three people of color have won Tonys for directing. What's wrong with the Tonys is what's wrong with Broadway. Without the vision of women and artists of color, audiences are seeing only the first act of the show.*

—*The Guerrilla Girls*[20]

Like a simian Darth Vader, I lead a troop of Guerrilla Girls in full-headed gorilla masks and flowing black capes down 51st Street. We

---

20 *New York Times,* June 4, 2000.

turn at Fifth Avenue. Stomps and claps are heard up the avenue from the south as nine women and two men in cheerleading skirts, fishnet stockings, and boots approach. They are the Art Cheerleaders. We face off and a crowd gathers.

> *WELCOME TO THE GREAT WHITE WAY!*
> *WHERE WHITE GUYS WRITE ALL THE PLAYS!*
> *HEY, HEY! HO, HO! SEXIST BROADWAY'S GOT TO GO!*

Armed with paper-bag masks with a gorilla mask/face on one side and "I'm a Guerrilla Girl" on the back, we ease in and out of the crowd, pass the bags out, and instruct the public to slip them over their heads and join in the chanting. A Saint Patrick's Cathedral security guard swoops down.

— You are blocking the entrance to the church. If you don't get out of here I'm calling the cops!

I imagined a huge congregation of people wearing paper-bag masks, along with black-caped gorilla-masked women and a group of short-skirted cheerleaders descending on Radio City Music Hall. Our energy and anger would turn the cameras and the reporters away from the Tony nominees and focus on us and our goals. The press would write compelling reports of our plight that would sizzle over the airwaves. The Tony Awards would be suspended while the entire theatre community convened to assure that women and people of color were never excluded again.

At least one hundred masks are gone, some to people who simply grab them as if they are handouts for a nearby warehouse sale of discounted suits and walk off. The people who show up to protest slip them over their heads and we all take off for Radio City Music Hall chanting:

> *HEY, HEY! HO, HO! DISCRIMINATION HAS GOT TO GO!*

Crossing 51st Street in an orderly line, we are a group of fifty or so, in paper-bag masks, gorilla masks, and cheerleading outfits. People stop and stare. One gorilla-masked woman shoves a poster into the hands of a stranger. She stops to read it.

KNOW YOUR THEATRE LINGO:

- **Plot** \plät\ *n.* White guy writes play; it gets produced.

- **Subplot** \səb-,plät\ *n.* Less than 18% of plays produced in the U.S. this season were written by women or people of color.*

- **Farce** \färs\ *n.* Last season was just as bad.

- **Tragedy** \traj-əd-é\ *n.* The lack of diversity in theatre.

*SOURCE: *Amercian Theatre* Season Preview issue, Oc

As we reach Radio City we jockey for prime position and secure a space right in front of the artists' entrance. An NYPD officer steps up and addresses our group.

— Who's in charge here?

— I am, I reply. We are protesting sexism on Broadway. Did you know that women don't win Tonys because . . .

— Fine. But you have to stand behind the barricade.

NYPD officer Purtell cordons us off with a metal fence.

— Hey, we are getting our own cage! Lorraine Hansberry cries out! Yeah!

Cheers go up.

— Another thing, the masks have to come off.

Officer Purtell cites a law passed during the height of the Ku Klux Klan. No one can protest in a mask. I attempt to explain the importance of not showing our faces in public.

— Between you and me, if you just get all those people with paper bags on their heads to show their faces you should be fine.

No one has ever heard of the law. The white paper-bag masks were maybe not the best choice of a look. The people in paper-bag masks take them off and turn them into hats or hand puppets. Fans, waiting to see a Broadway star, snicker at us as tourists snap photos and video cameras whir. *THE TONY IS BALONEY!*

We are very, very loud thanks to the Art Cheerleaders, who have their act down. A frustrated reporter from CNN approaches the barricade and begs me to shut our group up for five minutes so she can videotape a short report. She promises to interview us if we will just be quiet. Politely, we comply. When she sticks the microphone up to my mouth for a statement afterward, I know she probably does not even have it turned on.

— We are here because women and people of color do not win Tony Awards because they do not work on Broadway. They do not call it the Great White Way for nothing.

I do believe the CNN reporter rolls her eyes at me but I cannot tell from inside my mask. As soon as she wraps up our interview and drags her cameraman away from us I spot a man in a tuxedo approaching. He is the producer of the PBS segment of the Tony Awards and wants to know what the hell is going on. I shove a poster into his hand, push my rubber mask up to his face, and repeat what I said to the CNN reporter.

— You have it all wrong! he cries. The Tonys don't discriminate. You've picked the wrong people. We are not responsible for sexism. You know, I used to like the Guerrilla Girls, but now I don't.

— But women and people of color do not win Tonys because . . .

He is gone. *HEY, HEY! HO, HO!*

Suddenly, Alec Baldwin steps out of a limo. He smiles, waves, and once he notices us, his face goes blank. He begins to shoo away the people who surround him and push across the street.

Oh my God, Alec Baldwin is headed in my direction!

The Guerrilla Girls rush together, each one of us eager to speak to Alec Baldwin. We shove posters and stickers into his hands and explain as best we can, through our rubber masks, exactly what we are doing here. He nods, asks a few questions, and promises to look into it. Then he turns and heads back across the street.

ALEC BALDWIN! ALEC BALDWIN!

A wild chant begins for Alec Baldwin. Dame Edna pulls up in a pink convertible. More Broadway stars arrive. No one even looks our way. I see a man from a theatre company I previously worked for walk down the street in a tuxedo with a bouquet of roses in his hand. Ha! He has no idea it is me behind this mask! As he walks by I chant loudly, *HEY, HEY! HO, HO! RACIST BROADWAY'S GOT TO GO!*

Journalist Sue Halpern scribbles on a pad and works the crowd, looking for people to interview. She will write an article about our protest for *Mother Jones.*

The Guerrilla Girls, The Art Cheerleaders, and the Guerrilla-Girl-For-A-Day protesters hold each other up, convinced we are making an important point and hopeful that our actions will have impact.

I stray from my focus for a minute to fantasize. *And the Tony Award for best protest goes to . . . The Guerrilla Girls. And the Tony Award for best play goes to . . . Aphra Behn! And the Tony Award for lifetime achievement in the theatre goes to . . . Donna Kaz! Put me on Broadway! Give me a Tony!*

Just as I grab the Tony in my dream, step up to the mic, and am about to thank the American Theatre Wing, NYPD's chief of patrol for the Borough of Manhattan South arrives.

— You have five minutes to take off your masks or be arrested.

All of us had discussed this moment. Our IDs and credit cards were in our pockets. Someone was standing by to post bail. After a short discussion we decide to leave. It is not worth getting arrested.

And just as quickly as the protest seemed to come together, it dissipates. We turn and head back toward Saint Patrick's Cathedral, chanting as loudly as ever as we disappear down the street. *HEY, HEY! HO, HO! HEY, HEY! HO, HO!*

The Tony Awards go on as planned. Three out of the four nominees in the Direction of a Musical category are women. None of them win.

13

1980, MALIBU TO NEW YORK CITY

THE FILMING OF *ALTERED STATES* IS over. Along with Blair and a few crew members, we host a big wrap party at the beach.

Bill's next job is to play Hamlet at Circle Rep. He purchases a brand-new Honda that we will drive across the country to get home.

I turn twenty-five years old. We celebrate with Richard Jordan at Moonshadows restaurant in Malibu. Blair is off on another job.

Even though I know going back to New York City means I will finally be able to pursue a career, make my own money, see my family, I stand on the bungalow deck and cry the day before we leave. There is something final about the end of my life in Malibu. Here I had boundaries and limitations. The bungalow was a sort of gorgeous prison. I am being set free and have no clue as to what will happen next. I suppose if all else fails, I can always get a job as a water safety instructor.

In a rare moment of clarity, Bill and I agree that our relationship needs work and we should not live together once we get back to New York City. I am relieved we are not breaking up. I have a vision of my life with Bill that I am determined to make work. Fortified by his assurances that I am his true love, I will not loosen my grip on my dream.

He swears to make our relationship better and I promise to get my own place as soon as we return to New York.

We pack all of our belongings into the Honda and carve out a space for Bats in the back seat. Our plan is to head north first. In Big Sur we run into two members of the *Altered States* crew for a wild night of drinks, drugs, and an endless exchange of stories about the making of the movie. We hit San Francisco and connect with friends of Bill's from American Conservatory Theater. We continue north to Bill's mother's grave.

— This is Donna.

Bill addresses his mother's spectacular grave, surrounded by land and sky in the middle of nowhere.

— Hello.

I have never spoken directly to a grave before. Am I supposed to say more, introduce myself, throw a question out and wait, perhaps? Unsure, I walk back to the car so Bill can have a moment alone with his mom.

We spend that night with relatives of Bill's. In the morning they serve us up fried eggs with homemade venison sausage. We have gone as far north as we can. It is time to begin the long road east to New York.

Somewhere around here I pick up a message on my answering service from the Performing Garage. They need a box-office manager and want to hire me. I exhale a sigh of relief about work. I will be employed when I return to New York.

As soon as we hit Milwaukee, Bill tells me he is late for *Hamlet* rehearsals and must get on a plane bound for New York City right away. He asks me to take him to the airport and drive the Honda and Bats the rest of the way home.

I am nervous about doing this, but I find hotels to stay in where I can sneak Bats in for the night. Behind the wheel of the Honda I drive over the George Washington Bridge and into Manhattan in late October of 1979. I will stay with Bill, as we agreed, until I can find my own apartment.

Bill arranges for me to audition for the Circle Rep Lab, a group of actors, writers, and directors who meet regularly in a workshop. I work on a short scene with a friend, and when the audition comes I am convinced I have blown it. I remember being so relaxed and calm during my performance that there can be no way I was any good. I did nothing on the stage. I was just myself.

That night, at Bill's apartment, he tells me the people from Circle Rep who attended my audition loved it. I was real. I was a natural. I am surprised, assuaged, and pleased. However, this is just a preliminary audition. I have to repeat the audition for Marshall W. Mason, the artistic director of Circle Rep, to actually be asked to join the Lab.

A friend from college hooks me up with an apartment in his building on West 89th Street, a real New York City Upper West Side score. It is a rent-stabilized, one-bedroom walk-up with a fireplace, high ceilings, and a terrace. The rent is $285 a month. I do not know how I am going to manage to pay that much money, but I take the leap and sign the lease on January 1, 1980.

Bill cannot handle Bats anymore. He is too busy, never home during the day, and performing every night. He asks me to find her a new home. It does not take me long. I have a friend who has been looking for a dog and agrees to adopt her. Bats is not quite one year old.

Not long after that, I bump into the friend on the street. As soon as he sees me he begins to cry. He tells me Bats was hard to walk. She would lunge at other dogs and growl. He felt he could not handle her so he took her to a shelter to be adopted. When she came through the doors of the shelter she leapt up and tried to bite the receptionist. The shelter told him she was unadoptable and would have to be put down. He left her there.

Bats, witness to rage, a receiver of violence and abuse, the amazing Frisbee-catching dog, was gone. I sobbed with my friend because I failed her. I wept because she was all the family I had in California. She looked after me the best she could and I did not protect her in return.

Even now, after all these years have passed, I think about Bats almost every day. I regret most not doing more for her. I should have done more. I should have done so much more.

On the sidewalk with my friend all I can do is to send up my love and gratitude to her in a prayer of thanks. I close my eyes and see her obediently sitting on the beach, waiting for us to swim to shore and take her home. She will never feel pain again. Bats is finally free.

↯

Back at the Performing Garage, the Performance Group is now the Wooster Group, and I am their box-office manager. Spalding Gray does not recognize me the first time I see him. The next time we meet he has decided it is because I look "California-ized." The box-office job alone will not pay the rent on my new apartment, so I put my apron back on and work brunches at an Irish pub in Turtle Bay. Another friend turns me on to seasonal work at a jewelry boutique near my apartment. I put my recent Red Cross water safety instructor certificate to use as a part-time lifeguard and swimming instructor at a health club on the Upper West Side. Lastly, Bill hires me to clean his apartment twice a month.

I need the money, so why not? He may earn a substantial salary while I live paycheck to paycheck, but what difference does that make? I wish to be financially independent and need the work.

Bill hires me as his housekeeper and also generously pays for my Linklater voice technique classes with Clyde Vinson, one of the leaders of the Circle Rep Lab. That makes up for him paying me to clean his apartment, correct? Or does it? Something about the whole arrangement never feels right.

↯

Bill's agents start to work with me and once or twice a month set up an audition. It is a trial run—they put me out there to see how I do. If I do well they might sign me. The pressure is huge. At the Public Theater, aka the New York Shakespeare Festival, Bill's agents arrange for me to do a general audition—two contrasting monologues. In the middle of my comedic speech, the head of Public Theater casting, Rosemary Tischler, slips in through a side door to watch me. After it is over I wait for Bill's agents to tell me what Rosemary thought. They never do. I must have bombed. After that, every time the agents send me out, I am my old bursting bubble of nerves.

Yet 1980 is a time of tremendous self-growth and education for me. I am exposed to the experimental theatre work of Mabou Mines, discover books by Doris Lessing, compose songs on my guitar, and fill notebooks with poetry and essays. No longer isolated, I rekindle old relationships with friends I met before I left for Malibu. And I meet new people.

Through Bill I meet a man who becomes my closest artistic ally, the biggest supporter of my work, and my greatest friend.

Charles T. Harper is a member of Circle Rep, and we meet at a lunch during rehearsals for *Hamlet* (he played Reynaldo). While Bill chats with Tanya Berezin, one of the founders of Circle Rep, Charles and I find out we have everything in common. He studied tap dancing as a child, was raised Catholic, plays the guitar, and has an intense comedic edge.

As we laugh our way through lunch a strong bond is forged between us. It feels as though we have known each other for a very long time. My deepest love may be for Bill, but something as profound exists with Charles from the moment we are introduced.

At the opening-night party for *Hamlet,* I appreciate just how excellent a dancer Charles is. We spend the entire night connected, first via the jitterbug and, as the evening evolves, in the execution of a free-spirited physical improvisation. Without a care of who watches us, Charles and I perform an interpretive dance all over the *Hamlet* set.

For me it feels like two geniuses have collided and the result is the spontaneous creation of some brilliant choreography. In the years to come we would lift our spirits whenever we felt blue by tap-dancing duets à la Astaire and Rogers.

We are able to quickly establish a deep friendship because Bill does not mind the time or attention I spend on Charles. Charles is gay and Bill prefers to be locked in an intellectual debate with one of his peers than to dance with me anyway.

Charles lives ten blocks north of me on the Upper West Side. With Bill often occupied in the evenings, Charles and I spend almost every night together. A six-pack of beer and a simple dinner prepared by us both is followed by hours of music, song, dance, and conversation.

Because Charles grew up on a farm in upstate New York, he has country music in his veins and he introduces me to Loretta Lynn, Hank Williams, Johnny Cash, and Merle Haggard. We both own old Gibson guitars and while one of us strums, the other sings. He encourages me to learn the repertoire of Patsy Cline and works out intricate backup harmonies.

In retrospect, country music became an outlet for my inner turmoil and Charles and I came to depend on both the music and each other to provide a release from the strains of our lives. We were two artists grappling with making ends meet and finding ways to express ourselves. Charles longed to be in relationship. I was hooked on a toxic love. We reached deep into our souls and interpreted songs about falling to pieces and sweet dreams that would never come true with a singular honesty.

These serious moments between us are always interrupted by our mutual love for absurdity and our search for the bliss of invention. Our senses of humor line up exactly. We get each other's jokes and puns and often spend whole evenings as alter egos, acting out a couple of wild characters we had invented. When *Coal Miner's Daughter* is released we watch and re-watch it until we can recreate entire scenes, me as Loretta Lynn, and Charles playing her husband, Doolittle.

If the humor, the music, and the dance are not enough to adhere us together, we also discover we both believe the art of acting is something spiritually based. We spend hours discussing the connection between the soul and imagination.

After *Hamlet,* Bill is cast in the movie *Eyewitness* with Sigourney Weaver. Bill and I see each other as much as we can, which only means we spend the night in the same bed. I let myself into his apartment with the set of his keys he has given me and wait. Many times he does not show up until the early morning with the weakest of excuses. *I passed out and the director took me home to sleep,* or my personal favorite, *I was night shooting.* When he comes in at 5 a.m. or 7 a.m., I am asleep in his bed. I wake when I hear his key go in the lock and turn my face to see his outline in the frame of the bedroom door. He wears the same clothes from the day before, his hair is wet from a recent shower, the scent of an odd brand of shampoo in the air. His first words are always a denial that he has been untrue. He will swear up, down, across, and sideways that all roads lead to me, I am the only one and there is no one else. I have no energy to resist him for long. I reach out my hand, fall back into bed, drag him down beside me, place my palm on his forehead, swipe it down to close his eyelids and cover his mouth to stop him from rattling on so he can rest before the sun comes up and he has to go back to work.

I would not be surprised to find out that he was juggling multiple relationships with other women, using the same excuses he swore to me. Every day he strays more and more. He disappears for twenty-four hours once. Yet he never admits he has been with another woman. Instinctually, I know he has. The violence between us does not stop.

Charles fills the parts of my life Bill cannot. I am not invisible when I am with Charles. I am whole. Charles will pick up his guitar and with a nod of his head, encourage me to belt out the lead of a song. If I consider Bill as my one true love, Charles is my soul mate. We often talk about how we must have known each other in a past life.

We devise a plan to make theatre together. I show Charles some of my writing, stuff I have never shown anyone before.

— Why, you are a playwright, honey.

Charles has this initial reaction to my work. I have not contemplated writing plays before, but with his help I find a voice inside my pages. He shapes those pages into my first play, which he directs as a small production in his big apartment. The process of collaborating with Charles is seamless and organic. I am a playwright.

Yet, I never tell Charles about the abuse I experience while it is happening to me. I tell only one person about it while it is going on, my friend from college who lives in Santa Monica. If there are black-and-blue marks on my wrists I wear long-sleeved shirts. With the exception of the broken finger, all of my bruises are hidden by my clothes. I cannot admit to myself my reality, so how could I let anyone else in on my secret? I furtively hope one day it will vanish and I will never have to speak of it at all.

After it is over, I tell Charles everything. His response is to hold me and let me cry for as long as I need to. I cry on his shoulder for hours. Sometimes he would take me in his arms once each day, as I made attempts to exorcise myself from the dark unhappiness that gripped me right down to my marrow. I will not forget the day he put his hands on my shoulders, fixed his eyes on mine, and commanded me to stop the sobbing and move on with my life.

During the cold month of March, Bill finally has a break in his work schedule. He seeks out a place to go where no one knows him and finds a house to rent on an obscure island in the British Virgin Islands. He will spend a week there by himself before I fly down to join him.

I find out my second Circle Rep Lab audition is scheduled for one of the days I will be away. Reschedule it, he says. So I do.

I am late to the airport and race through the terminal just in time to slip through the plane door before the flight attendant closes it for takeoff. With all of my belongings in a carry-on satchel, I sleep during the entire flight. When I land in Tortola, I am supposed to look for a man who will escort me to a dock and a boat to the island. I assume it will be some sort of passenger ferry and am surprised to be met by a smiling man with a small boat big enough for just the two of us. We land on the shore of a very small isle where another man waits to drive me to the house that Bill has rented.

He is relaxed and tan but not very happy to see me. I think he regrets asking me to come. Maybe another woman just left? This thought goes quickly through my mind before I can stomp it out. With a fake smile I muscle up some inner strength, dump the contents of my satchel next to the bed, and suggest we go for a snorkel.

We do snorkel quite a bit as well as go deep-sea fishing, take walks on the beach, read books, drink cocktails, and eat dinner. We fight and make up. We sleep on opposite sides of the bed one night, make love the next. I pack some new sexy lingerie but when I put it on I feel invisible. I cannot shake the sense that Bill would rather either be alone or with someone else.

With no real supermarkets on the island, we place orders for food to be delivered from the mainland. One afternoon I take two steaks from the freezer and put them on the counter to thaw. When I go back to throw them in a frying pan I find only one of the steaks there. Out the back door, a mongoose skillfully drags one of our steaks into the hills. There goes my dinner. There goes me.

We will leave together, take the same flight back to New York City. As the day of our departure approaches, something happens that has never happened between us. Bill stops talking to me. I say something about something, again I miss exactly what it is I say or do, and when I ask Bill to explain he will not even look at me. Because we flew in on different flights our itinerary is not connected, so we have separate seats on the flight home anyway. We fly from Tortola to San Juan on opposite sides of the plane. Not once does he look over in my direction.

During a layover in San Juan I find Bill sitting at a bar and I beg him to talk to me. His angry fists have never been as painful to me as this absolute dismissal. He pretends I do not exist, and I have never felt more vulnerable in my life. If I open my mouth to speak, tears flow down my cheeks. I beg him to please say something. He will not even make eye contact. I do not exist. I have no idea what to do and feel as though I might go insane. Being in a strange airport alone becomes terrifying. I start to wonder if I will be able to pull myself together and get myself back to the city.

On the flight from San Juan to New York I see he is seated about ten rows ahead of me. I down a few vodkas and try to sleep during the flight. Just before we touch down, I feel a hand on my arm. It is Bill in the aisle, looking down at me with the expression I know so well: *please forgive me.* He has convinced the man next to me to change seats with him. We sit together as the rubber wheels of the plane touch the tarmac. He puts his arms around me and I am safe and home.

⚡

A letter is slipped under the door of Bill's apartment on an afternoon when we are both there. Bill reads the note and then hands it to me. It is from the single guy who lives right next door. In the letter the neighbor complains he can hear us yell and fight through the wall and vents. The noise disturbs him deeply.

The first time I read this I think, *We have been caught. Someone knows. Someone finally knows. Our violent New York City life is about to be exposed. Could help be on the way? Does this neighbor think I am in danger? Is he a Good Samaritan who is warning Bill to knock it off or he will tell someone about it, perhaps even call the police if he hears it again?*

I am embarrassed and excited at the same time. The only other time our fights have gone public is when the couple heard us as they drove by the bungalow in Malibu and stopped to pray with us. Now another person informs us they can hear the abuse through the walls. Will this neighbor shame Bill into stopping?

I read on. The neighbor outlines the details of what he thinks should be done. He proposes that Bill construct a wall between his kitchen and his living room so the neighbor no longer has to hear our fights. Regardless, he goes on to say that Bill must block the noise of his assaults immediately. If Bill does not want to build a soundproof wall, the neighbor suggests he will build one in his apartment and that Bill pay for it. The bottom line is, the sound of violence must not reach his ears ever again.

14

2001, NEW YORK CITY AND LOS ANGELES

IN THE DARKNESS, A VOICE:

Ladies and Gentlemen, please turn off your cell phones, beepers, and purse alarms. Guerrilla Girls On Tour! remind you that in most theatres, the taking of photographs, the use of a recording device, and the production of plays by women is strictly prohibited. If any woman in the audience should experience a sudden hot flash, please stand up and let us know. Guerrilla Girls On Tour! pause for hot flashes, menstrual cramps, contractions less than two minutes apart, and sudden attacks of osteoporosis. Thank you.[21]

— Why don't we write a play? If the history of women in theatre is not included in the history books, why don't we write a play about it?

I propose this question to Lorraine Hansberry one day while we meet for coffee to talk about future Guerrilla Girl actions. As Guerrilla Girls we make posters about the current state of art. Why not write a play about the current state of theatre?

---

21 From "Feminists Are Funny," by Aphra Behn and Guerrilla Girls On Tour!

In 2000, Lorraine Hansberry and I write a grant proposal to the New York State Council on the Arts to research and write *The History of Women in American Theatre.* To our knowledge, there is no book or play that gives a comprehensive overview of the thousands of women who have helped shape the American theatre into what it is today.

For example, the previous year, *The Cambridge History of American Theatre* was published. While it contains three references to the 1922 long-running Broadway hit *Abie's Irish Rose,* there is no mention in the book of the author of the play. Anne Nichols spent five thousand dollars of her own money to stage her work, *Abie's Irish Rose,* and wound up a millionaire when it ran for 2,327 performances, becoming at the time the longest run in Broadway theatre history. Left out of *The Cambridge History of American Theatre* is Anne Nichols's name, and the names of many other women of theatre who came before us, as well as their vast achievements. They shall be featured in our play.

We get the NYSCA grant and follow up with an application to A.S.K. Theatre Projects' annual Common Ground Festival, a theatre program in Los Angeles that supports new plays with developmental assistance. A.S.K. invites us to participate in their 2001 Common Ground Festival.

We are jazzed to tackle a play about the history of women in American theatre, then we realize that information on all these missing theatre women will be hard to find. We scan the Internet, libraries, out-of-print books, and journals, and from our search we decide to limit our play to works by women playwrights, no longer living, who wrote plays in English to be performed on a raised stage. (Apologies for excluding the performance traditions, rituals, and religious ceremonies of Native American women.)

The two of us divide the work and the playwrights between us and cobble together a first draft and then another after a table reading of it at the A.S.K. offices a few months before the festival. We decide to perform the play ourselves, and add Hallie Flanagan as a third character, a device we hope will keep the play moving forward.

Our play is an overview of the lives of almost twenty American theatre women whose work addresses identity, gender, race, class, age, and/or ethnicity. From Mercy Otis Warren, to Pauline Elizabeth Hopkins, to Angelina Weld Grimké, to Fanny Brice, Anne Nichols, Alice Childress, Lorraine Hansberry, and Dorothy Fields, we find so many similarities in themes, styles, and individual life stories that it often feels as if we are simply telling and retelling the same story over and over. "One woman's herstory is every woman's herstory" is a line we include in the show.

The best part of the Common Ground Festival experience is being introduced to a mask designer, who takes the Guerrilla Girl moniker Bessie Potter Vonnoh.[22] Bessie has the brilliant idea to reconceptualize our masks and make them more performance-friendly. She suggests we ditch the full-head rubber gorilla masks we have always worn and substitute wigs and half gorilla masks in their place. The half masks can be changed for other half masks during performances. Bessie purchases two voluminous black hair wigs and designs and builds new rubber half masks—a gorilla/comedy one for me and a gorilla/tragedy one for Lorraine. Beneath these masks we wear a basic black mask to cover our faces while we switch out to other masks like those of a young girl, old woman, or middle-aged man during the performance.

This is the start of my unmasking. With my lower face exposed, my facial expressions are no longer hidden from view. You see me smile, frown, shout, or laugh out loud. As a performer, I can better establish a connection with the audience. This connection is what theatre would become all about for me as a Guerrilla Girl On Tour!

Since humor forms the base of our style, we turn ourselves inside out to find ways we can shove a bit of comedy into the play. Rachel Crothers wrote about divorce, Angelina Weld Grimké about the hopelessness of being black in America. Georgia Douglas Johnson

---

22 Bessie Potter Vonnoh (1872–1955), American sculptor, worked almost exclusively in bronze, known for small bronzes of domestic scenes.

addressed lynching, and Dorothy Fields turned to writing musicals after her father barred her from becoming an actress. Such serious themes lead to our writing a fractured play that aches to find humorous moments. We alternate historical facts with personal commentary and thus our theatrical celebration of the lives of women who established the tradition of women writing for the American theatre winds up as more a humbling conclusion of how difficult it had been for these women to merely live, let alone write. Even so, we are able to explore what a comedic and feminist performance style would look, feel, and sound like: part vaudeville, part parody. I would go on to develop that performance style as a Guerrilla Girl On Tour! As both an activist and playwright, dramatizing history is something I continue to tackle.

A.S.K., one of very few organizations dedicated to the development of new works, has since, unfortunately, shut its doors. Without it, Lorraine and I and a slew of other playwrights would not have experienced an important step in the creation of our plays.

During this time I am unanimously voted in as "gig girl" at a Guerrilla Girl meeting. My responsibilities are to field queries and book Guerrilla Girl "Gigs" at colleges, universities, and other venues. These bookings are the way the Guerrilla Girls earn the money to carry out our actions and print our posters.

With almost four years of Guerrilla Girl activism under my belt, it begins to be increasingly difficult to ignore the pushback and the backlash. Along with love letters, hate mail pours in. At performances the relationship between me, the Guerrilla Girl, and the audience is not always simpatico. During the Q-and-A we always add at the end of every appearance, there is usually one person who will ask, "Aren't there just more male artists than female artists?" "Aren't there just better plays by male playwrights than female playwrights?" Often there are complaints: "Why aren't you addressing sexism in music?" or "Why aren't there more women of color, LGBTQI women, women with disabilities in your group?" As a Guerrilla Girl I am accused of not being radical enough, of not covering all the issues, of male bashing, of making a spectacle of feminism. I am shaken when these retorts come from other women, which begins to occur with more and more frequency.

As Guerrilla Girl, Aphra Behn, I challenge the audience to take up the causes we do not have time to address and I encourage people to form activist groups of their own. We quash anti-male statements that have crept into our "Gig" script over the years and stress to the audience that we do not want the work of men to go away, we want equality. Diversity and inclusivity are important goals for our membership, and we try, not always successfully, to achieve them. We take questions and accusations seriously, spend time to research the numbers. No, there are not more male playwrights than there are female playwrights. We added up the number of women members of the Dramatists Guild, how many women have enrolled in college playwriting programs, and how many women make up the general population to come to that conclusion.

Behind the mask, as Aphra Behn, I learn that sometimes, no matter how much you try, you will not please those who think you should be funnier, further-reaching, and more feminist.

The number of Guerrilla Girls who show up at meetings dwindles. All of the energy generated at the retreat the year before sustains a very small number of active members. A disagreement crops up between the Girls about what direction we should take next. A few want to infuse the group with younger members, while others are more concerned with an equal number of women of color to white women members. Some Guerrilla Girls no longer want to work with other Guerrilla Girls.

Lorraine, Hallie, and I stay on the outside of most of these arguments. Our goals as Guerrilla Girls remain to focus on theatre with performances and plays that promote gender parity and diversity in theatre.

When you fight against something and see very little change it is easy to question whether you are doing any good. As Aphra Behn I sweat and grunt and put in hours of time to provoke the start of a dialogue about sexism in theatre within the theatre community. I hear very little discussion and see almost no change. Of course, change happens slowly, but with my own career to pursue, I question why am I wasting energy fighting something no one else in theatre seems to care about. The silence and same old, same old begins to take a toll on me. Suddenly, feminism is the "F" word, the entire movement is questioned, the past achievements regarded as no longer valid to women today.

For the first time, being Aphra Behn feels a little ridiculous. Then one very successful woman playwright confides to us that aligning herself with our cause is equivalent to career suicide. She cannot and will not openly support us.

I am accepted into the BMI Lehman Engel Musical Theatre Workshop as a book writer and lyricist. This eventually leads to a commission from a Broadway producer.

On July 29, 2000, I take the cast and crew of my own production of *JOAN* to the Edinburgh Festival Fringe. The show receives several positive reviews and, as a result, is written about in *American Theatre* magazine. It goes on to receive four additional productions.

On a balmy late summer night in New York City there is a terrible rainstorm. With Lorraine and Hallie, I sit in a coffee shop and we talk about our future as feminist masked avengers. As the rain smacks against the windows we all agree that the Guerrilla Girls theatre committee would function best as an independent organization and structured like a touring theatre company.

The torrential downpour suddenly clears away. Stars come out in a cloudless sky. The date is September 10, 2001.

15

1980, NEW YORK CITY, FLORIDA, AND LOS ANGELES

In August, my second Circle Rep Lab audition is finally rescheduled, almost nine months since the first one. I am supposed to repeat my original audition piece, but my scene partner is no longer around. I hustle to find someone to work with, and a friend suggests an actor I have no chemistry with. This should be fine since the audition is all about my work, not his, I think.

Charles works with us on the scene, from *The Woods* by David Mamet. I try to remember what I did nine months ago that was so spectacular, but I did not know what it was even then.

We arrive at the audition space, an oddly shaped room in Circle Rep's new offices. I perform the scene for Circle Rep's artistic director, Marshall Mason, and a few other company members, including Charles. In my heart I know I am not very good.

After it is over, Charles tells me the Circle Rep folks were in mid-discussion of my fate when the meeting suddenly had to break up because the room was scheduled for another event. A decision to let me into the Circle Rep Lab or not remains up in the air.

I cannot help but think it is all because my relationship with Bill is up in the air. A few months go by and I mention to Clyde Vinson, my voice teacher and head of one of the labs, that I still have not heard if I have been accepted. He tells me to just show up, so I do. Unfortunately the Circle Rep Lab will only last another few months. A huge restructure of the entire company will take place and I will be not be asked back to be a part of it.

Again, I feel my fate is more about how Circle Rep feels about Bill than about me. There is no risk of offending Bill if they reject me now, because we are no longer as solid a couple as we used to be. I should have done the callback when I could, closer to my original audition. I would have been accepted into the Lab and been able to establish myself there.

⚡

Bill is set to star in the movie *Body Heat*. He invites me to have dinner with the director, Lawrence Kasdan, and a few other people. I ask Bill if I can read the screenplay first. He shared the script for *Altered States* and his second movie, *Eyewitness,* with me. For some reason he is reluctant to give me the *Body Heat* script. I press him, remind him we should be able to share our work. Finally he flings the script at me from across the room with these words: "Read it and weep."

One of the first scenes in *Body Heat* involves Kathleen Turner's character, Matty, ordering Bill's character, Ned, to leave her house. He has come for sex, but she rebukes him and orders him to leave. He does leave, she locks the door, and he walks away. Suddenly he changes his mind, comes back to her door, picks up a chair, and smashes the window. He breaks into her house and has sex with her.

— Rape myth.

I have picked up the script from the floor and have just read the first scene.

— What?

— The first scene of this screenplay promotes a rape myth.

— No it does not.

— The woman clearly said "no." The guy breaks into her house and has sex with her. I mean, this implies women who say "no" don't really mean it. That promotes the myth that "no" really means "yes."

Bill and I begin a huge argument about this, in the middle of which we go off to have dinner with Lawrence Kasdan. We arrive at the restaurant first and are seated at a table, still in a clash about the script. Lawrence Kasdan appears and we stand up. Bill introduces me.

— This is my girlfriend, Donna. She thinks your screenplay is sexist.

Here comes a moving bus and there I go, in a head first slide across the asphalt under it. Lawrence Kasdan's eyes widen. He smiles at me and changes the subject. *Thanks, Bill,* I think to myself. I contribute very little to the conversation for the rest of the meal. Instead, I pick at my spaghetti and think up alternate opening scenes for *Body Heat:* Matty calls the cops and has Ned arrested. Matty is a karate master and drop-kicks Ned to the ground. Matty repeats over and over, no means no, until dumb Ned finally gets it.

$$\mathcal{L}$$

Body Heat shoots in Florida in November and Bill invites me to visit him for a week. I clearly remember choosing some new, nonfiction feminist manifesto to read on the plane and tossing a black felt beret into my bag. Once Bill spots me in the black hat he remarks that I look like I am ready for a revolution. Maybe my new, feminist resolve gives him the courage to follow up this remark with a confession. He and his costar, Kathleen Turner, have had a short fling.

I always knew, in my heart, that Bill was unfaithful. Every time I called him on it he denied it, however. He never, ever told me the truth about his digressions.

My first reaction to his declaration of guilt is gratitude. He has been honest with me for the first time. I am happy. Who cares who he slept with—he told me about it! He must really trust me!

I see now how this moment solidifies me as a woman sinking far down into the numbing waters of denial. Maybe I can stand up against the distribution of rape myths, but I cannot comprehend how my own situation belittles and insults me as a woman. I am dead to the agony Bill inflicts on me. When I imagine him with someone else I topple over from the pain of it, yet at this moment I choose to see only the beauty of his honesty. I make a choice to shove aside his complete disregard for me as a human being and lavish him with praise for admitting his unfaithfulness. I have played the character of nobody in the scenario of our relationship so well I should win an Oscar.

Right after this exchange we head to Kathleen's hotel room for a drink. She falls on me with words of how much Bill talks about me and then pulls me into a corner of her suite and says:

— I just want you to know I never slept with Bill.

Now I have no words left inside. I smile, nod, try to appear grateful for this information and turn away to ask no one in particular for a dry martini straight up.

⚡

I am not surprised when Bill does not invite me to visit him on the set in Florida. I spend my time in a search for an escape from the soupy, hot weather. I take leisurely drives to the mall, where I window-shop and eat dinner alone. One day I find out that Bill has to work but Kathleen does not. She invites me to spend the day with her and her boyfriend, who also visits from New York. The three of us climb into a big rental car and drive aimlessly around Florida, Kathleen's boyfriend at the wheel, Kathleen in the passenger seat, and me in the back. The two of them turn around to talk to me as we roll along on a hunt for some hidden wonderful place in Florida to hang out for the day.

— Life without movies! Can you imagine what life would be like if there were no movies?

Kathleen's boyfriend stares at me in the rearview mirror. His wide eyes stress the profundity of his question.

— Sounds good to me.

I ponder how different my life would in fact be without movies and begin to chuckle. Kathleen turns her head back and laughs with me. Her boyfriend joins in and together we giggle and drive along the palm-tree-lined streets, in pursuit of a day without movies.

⚡

The end of 1980 approaches. Bill's agency makes an appointment for me to read for the movie *King of Comedy* starring Robert De Niro and Jerry Lewis. Terror and excitement fill my days in preparation for meeting the casting director, Cis Corman. As I work on the script I try to focus on just doing well instead of repeating over and over in my mind, *I have to get this job, I have to get this job, I have to get this job.*

On the day of the audition I arrive ten minutes early to Cis Corman's office in midtown. Not having read for a movie before, I am surprised to be led in to meet Corman herself. After a few minutes of talk, she picks up the script and invites me to read some scenes with her.

After every scene Cis looks up at me and says, "Good." I suppress the urge to pump my fist in the air and shout, *I am clicking with Cis Corman!* We read three scenes together before she stops and tells me she would like me to come back in a few weeks and read some other material.

Oh no. No, no, no! I am scheduled to go to LA with Bill for Christmas where he is finishing up *Body Heat.* I swallow hard. Should I tell her about my trip or should I just cancel it and schedule the callback? *I got a callback!* I quickly blurt out that I am scheduled to go away for the holidays but can change my plans. Cis tells me to go on my trip—she can schedule an appointment for me for when I get back. As she holds a stack of new pages out to me with an optimistic grin, I turn and leave her office with an appointment in January.

⚡

It is the first Christmas I have ever spent away from my family. The unrelenting sun of Los Angeles makes the freeways shimmer as the temperature jumps up and down, stretching into the nineties on Christmas Eve day. I was originally scheduled to return to New York City on December 30, 1980, but Bill convinces me to stay with him an extra week.

On Christmas morning he presents me with a goose-down explorer's jacket from Eddie Bauer. He mumbles a weak apology for his lack of ribbon and paper as he cheerfully bursts into the living room with the khaki-colored coat proudly held straight out in front of him.

— Do you like it? I bought myself the exact same one!

He runs back into the other room and emerges seconds later in an identical coat. I unzip the jacket and slip it on. It has two huge front outer pockets and a deep hood rimmed with coyote fur. The lining hugs my chest as I snap the front flap over the zipper. In the LA heat I begin to sweat, but I do not want to take the jacket off just yet. It is the most romantic thing he has given me since the tissue-wrapped pewter box with *Amo te* engraved on the bottom two and a half years ago. The coat is his way of enveloping me with protection and love, I think, as I grip the waist cord and draw it tight.

— Now for your present.

I slide a package from behind an overstuffed chair where I stashed it the night before. It is a new sienna-brown leather briefcase and took me weeks to pick out. After hitting every leather shop in Greenwich Village, I finally saw what I wanted in the window of a tiny store just off of Sixth Avenue. The case has two pockets and a simple stitched handle.

Bill uses an old and very worn-out leather briefcase whose seams are just about to burst. His initials are monogrammed on the front flap of the case, and something tells me a very special person presented it to him. In replacing his case, I hope to slip into the place that special person held in his life.

I crawl over to where he sits and place the package, wrapped in special gold paper, on his lap. He tears the paper off with the grab of one hand, thanks me with a peck on the lips, and puts the case aside.

He shoots up and onto his feet with a little hop and heads for the kitchen.

— Let's have breakfast. I'm starving!

As I slip four fried eggs onto two plates, I remind him I cannot stay until January 25, the date he is scheduled to fly back to New York.

— My callback for *The King of Comedy,* remember? The movie with Jerry Lewis and Robert De Niro?

— You can change the date of that, can't you?

— Maybe. But I don't want to change the date.

I do not want to change a date for an audition ever again.

— Besides, I want to prepare for it. I need time.

He does not understand about preparing for auditions. He is relaxed, confident, and, I imagine, able to waltz in and out of auditions with ease.

— Well, do what you need to do, I guess. I still wish you would stay with me until this is over.

A few months ago I would have stayed, I think, as I smear butter across a slice of toast. I used to love to hear that he needed me, that my physical presence was important to him. It is two weeks we will be apart. What could happen in fourteen days?

— I don't sleep well when you are not here, you know.

He reaches out and grabs my hand.

— Is your Christmas present okay? Do you like the briefcase?

— It's perfect.

⚡

We are staying in a rented house off of Laurel Canyon Boulevard, a small, split-level two-bedroom burrowed into the hills with an awning of eucalyptus trees suspended over the flat roof. The house comes with a compact black outdoor cat who appears every morning at the back door for food and then disappears for the rest of the day and night.

The owner of the house posts a note in the kitchen with a request that renters make sure the cat has food and water but not the name of this small, sweet creature. I pick up the cat's empty bowl and put the dishes in the sink.

After breakfast we drive down to the Laurel Canyon Country Store and pick up some wine. Then we take the Santa Monica Freeway west toward the Pacific Coast Highway. As we pass under the Santa Monica tunnel and emerge with a clear view of the azure-blue Pacific, we glance at each other and laugh out loud. I turn up the car radio up and sing to Supertramp's "Take the Long Way Home."

— Bill, let's drive up to the old bungalow.

— We don't have time. We're late.

— It's Christmas. How can we be late on Christmas?

He ignores me and takes a right into the Malibu hills. I close my eyes, think of the bungalow, and remember how I used to imagine I could feel the beach house shift on its pilings when the moon was full and the ocean raged.

After maneuvering our rented four-door over an unpaved road full of ruts and cutbacks, we arrive at Blair and Richard's and spend the afternoon drinking wine and playing darts in the yard. Blair has prepared a festive dinner of roast beef and Yorkshire pudding. It is just like old times and makes me nostalgic for the days when we lived so close to our good friends. We leave late and, once again, are lucky to make the drive home safely.

⚡

The following day we laze around the house and watch football. I look at the calendar and decide the last possible day I can return home is January 6. I pick up the phone, call American Airlines, and am put on hold. While listening to K-Earth 101 in the background, I picture myself cast in *King of Comedy*. I will star in a movie with Robert De Niro—Bob, I will call him Bob, like everyone else does. And Bill . . . well, how would Bill react? Will he honor his promise to support me and my career? Images of my face in the trailer of *King of Comedy* begin to vaporize and I close my eyes to try to conjure them back.

— Are you calling about a domestic or international flight? says a voice on the other end of the line.

We have dinner with some people from the *Body Heat* film crew that night, the gaffer and one of the camera operators and their girlfriends. I had never met them and the old uncomfortable feeling returns when they ask me what I do. The last and only time I had a job as an actress was almost two years ago.

— I have a callback for a film in a few weeks.

That sounds better, I think for a few seconds before I realize the correct answer is I do a lot of things, none of which are what I really want to do. I feel like such a loser. The gaffer smiles at me and nods blankly. The conversation at the table continues as I pull back, sip my wine, and observe for the rest of the night. On the car ride home, Bill accuses me of being too quiet. We argue. I defend my behavior but it sounds like what I try to defend is my very reason to exist.

The next few days I spend alone because Bill has to work. He leaves early, comes home late, and I fill the hours working on my audition sides and preparing dishes from an old cookbook I find in the kitchen. Sometimes I get in the car and drive around LA for hours. One day I head up the Pacific Coast Highway to see our old bungalow. I stop across the street from it and stare at the back gate and windows. It looks like no one is living there now.

One night, just before I am to return to New York, I say something and immediately want to stop the words from coming out of my mouth. I did not mean to say what I said. What I say flips a switch.

He turns on me, chases me around the house, finally catches up to me and throws me to the ground. I put up my arms up to protect myself from being slapped in the face and use my legs to kick him away. The bathroom remains the one place I know I will have temporary reprieve because I can lock the door. The lock clicks just as I reach safety. He pounds on the door, demands I open it. I crouch down in the shower and scream at the top of my lungs for him to stop.

He does stop, briefly. I check the lock, make sure it is secure. Suddenly, he changes his mind, comes back to the door, and begins to use his shoulder against it, like a battering ram. *Bam! Boom! Bam!* The screws in the hinges start to pull away from the frame. *Bam! Boom! Boom!* The wood of the door splinters as the screws and hinges pull out of the wall. *Boom! Bam! BOOM!* The door flies forward, dislodges the shower curtain rod, and hits me on top of the head. He pushes the door aside, grabs me by one arm and one leg, and drags me out of the bathroom and into the hallway, where he is down on top of me, slapping and punching and raging.

— No. No! NO!

Then, just as instantly as it began, he stands up and walks out of the house. I hear the car start in the driveway. It speeds away and when all is silent I pick myself up and wash my face.

⚡

The moment you think it cannot get any worse, it does. Two dozen roses. Making love in the gentlest and most delicate of ways. The words: Don't. Leave. Me. The confession: He is sorry. The myth: It will never happen again.

I know I speak no words, do no actions that deserve a violent response, that no action merits physical abuse. I am not a loser. Yet my identity is now all I have physically absorbed over the course of my relationship. I am what I have experienced.

⚡

On the morning of January 6, 1981, I stuff my new goose-down jacket into my suitcase. We have both gotten up before 6 a.m. because he has to work and my flight is at noon. Bill is being picked up by a studio car and has arranged for another driver to take me to LAX. As he rushes around the house, gathers up script pages, pops vitamins into his mouth, shoves cash into his pockets, I feed the little black cat and finish packing. He keeps stopping what he is doing to embrace me, to assure me how he will miss me. Since I have another three hours before I have to leave, I squeeze my suitcase shut, crawl back into bed, and close my eyes. I hear Bill's driver pull into the driveway.

— My driver is here.

He picks up his new briefcase in one hand and a large binder with his script in it in the other. The doorbell rings. I sit up in bed and am about to get out of it to say goodbye when he appears in the doorway and stands there, an outlined silhouette of a tall man holding a briefcase.

I reach out my arms to him, like a baby who wants to be lifted up. He walks to the side of the bed, places one knee on the mattress, and flops down right on top of me, his arms outstretched, one hand holds the briefcase to my right, the other holds the script to my left. With his arms occupied he nuzzles my neck.

— I love you, I love you, I love you.

I wrap my arms around him and rub his spine with my fingertips. Then I hold his face in my hands and kiss his lips.

— See you in two weeks. It will just be two weeks.

He rears back up onto his knees, his arms still laden with his briefcase and binder, rises off the bed, looks at me one last time, turns and bolts. The front door clicks shut.

I glance up at the ceiling, feel regret overtake me, and close my eyes. I become nostalgic for any period other than the recent past. Abruptly aware that I will never be able to rewind time, I open my eyes, and tears well up as though a mini garden soaker hose has been turned on underneath my eyelids.

Suddenly the cat, the tiny black cat who only comes for breakfast and never enters the house, is up on the bed, padding her way toward me. Tentatively, she places her small paw on the spot Bill just vacated and settles on my chest. I let out a sob as a soft purr hums from her belly. The vibration rattles the pool of tears cupped in my eyes and they drip over my cheeks and into my ears.

⚡

I land at JFK at 9 p.m. and take a cab to my apartment on West 89th Street. As I put my suitcase down I reach for the phone and call the number of the Laurel Canyon house. No answer. I look at my watch. It is just before 7 p.m. in Los Angeles. I pull the phone to one side of the bed and position it right next to my pillow. I brush my teeth and go to bed.

I wake with a start at 9 a.m. the next morning. I look at the phone, pick up the receiver, and check the dial tone. This is odd. He always calls me no matter what time it is. I have an appointment at the unemployment office at 11. Even though it is 6 a.m. in LA, I dial his number. No answer. I leave a message on his answering service, get into the shower, think he is probably at work already, that is all. He got home late and had to up early. He is busy. Before I leave my apartment I try him once more.

The unemployment office is cold and crowded. I fill out a form listing where I looked for work that week, wait on line for twenty minutes, and deliver the form to the clerk, who witnesses me sign my unemployment book. She pushes the book towards me, wishes me better luck this week, and sends me on my way.

I race home because I know he will have left me a message on my answering machine and I cannot wait to hear his voice. But there is no message. I pick up the phone, punch in his number, and leave another message on his service. Then I pace for fifteen minutes, while I imagine the worst possible scenario. He is gone. I call the house. I call again. And again every five minutes after that. I hang up when there is no answer and redial.

I do not hear from him all day. It is the first time in almost three years I have gone this long without some sort of communication with him. *Please call, please call, please call, please call,* I think over and over. I try to watch TV or read a book. I call Charles and we talk for a few minutes before I realize he may be attempting to get a hold of me at that precise moment and I am tying up the line. I tell Charles I will call him later and slam down the phone. My hand lingers on the receiver, ready to answer Bill's call.

The next morning I call Blair and Richard. No answer there either. For a moment I convince myself that phone service in the entire state of California is out. I call Blair's answering service and leave a message for her.

On day three I wake up crying. I let myself get hysterical for thirty minutes. Then I calm myself down with rational ideas of what could cause his behavior. He is busy. He is working. After work he is out with a director or a cast member or the crew until all hours of the morning. The three-hour time difference has made us miss each other's calls. He is very, very tired, and will fall asleep and forget to call. He is in a black pool of darkness. As soon as he emerges he will call.

I feel much better after I envision every excuse and possible positive scenario. I get myself together for a voice lesson that afternoon. As I squeak through "Baubles, Bangles, and Beads," the song my teacher assigned me, I stop to blurt out that I hate the song and ask for another. He hands me "The Party's Over."

On the walk home I try to move casually and slough off thoughts that I may soon face the world on my own. If I keep calm the earth will turn and all will be fine. Still, I cannot help but add up the number of hours we have not been in touch. It is more than any other time. I go over every moment of the days we spent together in LA for clues to why he would cut me off like this, but I come up with nothing. In the past he surfaced just when I thought I would lose my mind. I am way past that point now. With the belief he would never just disappear lodged in my body, I hold on to anything I can invent to keep this as something we both will recall at a later date and find amusing.

He always comes back. He will come back.

Then Blair calls.

— I haven't spoken to him either. I'll see if I can locate him and call you if I do.

Blair is kind, reassuring, and I relax into her words.

The weekend arrives. I go out to Long Island to spend time with my mom and dad. I reveal nothing about how I have not heard from Bill in four days. My mother asks how Christmas in LA was and I show her the goose-down jacket he gave me as a gift. After everyone is in bed I sneak into the living room and dial his number.

On Sunday night I return to New York City. I have still not heard from him. As soon as I walk in the door of my apartment I pick up the phone and leave a desperate, pleading message on his service.

— I (gulp) don't (sniff) know (gulp) why (sniff) you (gulp) are doing this to me! Please, please call, I am begging you!

My voice cracks and moans. I know it sounds ugly but I do not care.

On Monday I have my callback for *King of Comedy*. Again, I meet with Cis Corman in her office. I am determined not to let the events of the previous week distract me or influence my work. I will turn every-thing around and use my sorrow to shore me up. *I will show him,* is all I can think of while reading scenes with Cis.

Again, Cis stops only to give her direction and encouragement. After each scene she puts down her pages, peers over her reading glasses, and looks me right in the eye and says, "Good!" The callback lasts fifteen minutes. When it is over I am more than relieved.

I call my agent, his agent, and tell him how it went. I do not talk about Bill at all. The last thing I want is for the agent to know that Bill and I are in crisis.

That night I sit on my beige sofa and look out the tall windows in my living room at the bare sumac tree behind my brownstone and my phone rings. I place my hand over the phone and count two rings before I grab the receiver out of the cradle.

It is Blair and Richard, Blair on the main phone, Richard on the extension in their bedroom in Malibu. They start by telling me how much they love me and how grateful they are to have me as a friend. It feels like my parents have called to tell me my sister has been hit by a car.

— We have some news. We want you to hear it from us. Last night we went to a party. Bill was there. He wasn't alone. He had a woman with him.

I listen as Blair describes every detail, anxious for her to get to the point.

— We never met her before. He introduced us and we really did not spend any time talking to them at all, because he said she was his new girlfriend.

There. Blair has said it. It is official. It is over. Someone else has replaced me. I move my body up on the sofa so I can hunch into a ball over the phone.

— Are you sure? Really sure?

This is all I can think of to say, to ask them if they maybe heard wrong.

— Yes. We called you because we are sure. We actually only said one other thing to him, and that was to ask him what happened with you. He didn't have an answer.

They want me to hear it from them, not from the newspaper, not from anyone else. They agree he is an asshole for doing this to me in this way, for not telling me straight, for disappearing. They remind me I did nothing wrong.

Blair and Richard ask if I am okay. Richard says he is very sorry. Blair says she is angry. Everyone on the line feels betrayed.

I talk to them for another thirty minutes. We discuss possible missed signs and come to the only rational and mature conclusion we can: it is all for the best. Blair and Richard will be in New York in February. They promise to see me then.

— Until then, if you need us we are here for you.

— Call anytime.

Blair adds, "We love you," before they both hang up.

I put the receiver back in the cradle, grab my goose-down jacket, and head for the door. Once I get to the street I march the thirteen blocks south to Bill's apartment and use the keys he gave me to let myself in.

When I turn on the light and look around I half expect something to be different. The slipshod bookshelves I had dusted every two weeks still hold his stereo, the wires still trail down to two speakers set on the floor. The exposed brick wall still leads to three curtainless windows overlooking West End Avenue. The quilt on his bed is untouched. The bathroom towels are fresh and unused.

I push a button on the stereo and 104.6 FM comes on with a song I do not recognize. Over at the window, I look down at West End Avenue. The streetlamp illuminates a couple walking hand in hand. I reach down to touch his black leather Eames chair. I suddenly realize I am trespassing and robotically move through the apartment to collect the few items I keep there: a couple of T-shirts, the Swiss Army knife he gave me, my toothbrush, a tube of contraceptive gel. In five minutes I am finished.

In the middle of his small, one-bedroom apartment I struggle with what to do next. I feel a bubble in my belly. It expands and floats up through my lungs, pushes air into my cheeks, which begin to quiver. I open my mouth and let out a fluff of sound, a choked cry I immediately attempt to swallow back into myself. I think of Bill's snotty next-door neighbor, listening at the vents. Who cares about him now? My core is filled with air, and as I open my mouth the grief comes out like a paper horn on New Year's Eve.

A bright light flashes through the windows. Someone across the street has turned on a lamp. Not wishing to be seen knocks me off balance. I sink down to the floor. The polished wooden slats feel alive, they pulsate and for a moment I imagine I am back in our Malibu bungalow with the ocean rising around me.

I shove the few items I collected into the deep front left pocket of my coat. I try to stand but am knocked over by a wave of memory. He is in the kitchen making coffee, in the Eames chair reading a book, on the deck just after a swim, crumpled on the linoleum, watering the geraniums, stepping out of the shower, running down the beach. My memory is made even stronger by the robust scent of hibiscus, lemon oil, sea sand, and cedar wafting through the room. His scent. At that moment a wave crashes below me, the ocean lifts the floor up and begins to suck me out to sea.

I pull the hood of my coat over my head and tighten the draw-string around my chin. I try to stand up but I feel the floor rock violently forward. The sea opens up and swallows me. I fall downward into a spiral of cold, salty water toward a murky green light. I am jolted by the shudders of my own body gasping for breath when suddenly I hear music come from the radio with a familiar song.

Little darlin'. Someone is singing the words "little darlin'," and about a long, cold, lonely winter.

The song steers my mind away from the storm in my chest and helps me will myself into calmness. Yes, there are no coincidences in life. The singer on the radio is singing for me. I am his little darlin'.

I rip the hood off my head and pull the flap covering the zipper of my coat. The coat unzips easily and I draw out one arm, then the other, and fling it off and onto the floor.

And just at that moment I rise from the murky green waters and shoot up like Flipper, like a mermaid, like a synchronized swimmer going for Olympic gold. I inhale deeply, right down through the backs of my knees, into the heels of my sneakers, my breath sucked straight down and through the floor. My gasp reaches its deepest limit, bounces up and out and blows away the fog.

It is a warm coat, a nice coat. He will never get the foolish message of spite I attempt to send if I leave it here.

I scoop the coat up into my arms and head for the door. My right hand palms the lights off with a snap as I step into the hallway.

I slam the door shut, lock both the top and bottom locks, and then trip skillfully down the stairway, out the front door, and onto the street.

When I am a block away I remember I forgot to turn the stereo off.

I do not go back.

Here comes the sun.

16

1981–89, NEW YORK CITY AND LOS ANGELES

IT IS OVER. EXCEPT IT IS not.

I finally make contact. Bill agrees to meet me for lunch. Everything I want to say to him I write down because I suspect I will never get the chance to speak to him again. I bring the notebook full of questions with me. "What happened, who is she, are we done?" Bill shows up late and has no answers for me except to say he needs time. I ask him if he still loves me. He does not know. He needs time. I ask him what he is telling other people about us. He says nothing. He needs time. I ask him if he is seeing someone else. He does not think so. He needs time.

We order food, which I barely touch because I silently weep on and off through the ordeal. At the end he stands up, gives me a hug, and leaves.

Somewhere deep inside of me I grasp that the right thing to do would be to end it now. His idea of breaking up is to keep his options open. Because of this I hang on to the thin and frayed line that connects us to each other.

If I imagine a future without him a flood breaks through my gimcrack heart and I weep until I am completely squeezed dry, not a drop of liquid left inside. I feel brittle, wasted, and deprived of strength.

Even if I do not see him for a while, he is everywhere I go. His face blown up on billboards, in newspaper ads; his photo in magazines; his voice on the television or radio. I go to great lengths to get away from the world he dominates and sign up for a whitewater rafting trip in a remote national park. When my guide finds out I am an actor, he only has one question: Did I ever see the movie *Altered States*?

In April we spend the night together in my apartment. We continue to spend nights together once, twice, sometimes three times a year after that, occasionally going years with only a few phone calls or letters between us. I hold the hope in my belly that a switch will flip one day and we will get back together for good. We pretend we are two really good friends. He is never violent again.

$$\nmid$$

1981: I audition for the Women's Experimental Theatre. They ask me why I want to be in a feminist theatre company. I say because I genuinely feel oppressed. I am cast in their showcase production of "Food." The *Village Voice* writes in their review of the show that I am "especially good."

1982: I return to waitressing, land a job at the brand-new and hip Saloon restaurant directly across from Lincoln Center where some waiters work the floor in roller skates (not me). My boss is a foul-mouthed tyrant whose favorite comment to the women on the wait staff is to tell us our "tits are shrinking." I feel some vindication when I put my tips into an account at the First Women's Bank, the first woman-owned commercial bank in New York City.

1983: I receive a phone call from Bill with news. He is a father.

I write my first play for five actors based on the writings in notebooks I have kept since high school. Charles directs the play and stages it in his apartment.

I audition to understudy Kathy Baker in *Fool for Love* at Circle Rep. Once again I rely on my old audition technique and let my angry bitch self out, unable to tap into an ounce of openness.

1984: I attempt to organize the Saloon waiters into joining the union. The owners discover my plot and offer everyone health insurance. The union is overwhelmingly voted down.

When Geraldine Ferraro is nominated for Vice President I watch her deliver her acceptance speech on television and sob with hope as she eloquently vows to pass the Equal Rights Amendment.

My second play is picked up for development by a small production company. My downstairs neighbor and college buddy, Marc, suddenly gets sick and dies of the newly discovered disease AIDS.

1985: I enroll in school to learn the healing art of shiatsu massage. At the Saloon it seems as if every week some waiter does not show up for their shift and soon after is dead from AIDS.

I quit the Saloon and find work with a film production company, reading scripts and writing coverage.

Charles and I form a country band and perform downtown.

1986: I am awarded a writing residency at the artists' colony Yaddo and spend a month in Saratoga Springs. Immediately after, I score my first production job, as the third assistant director on a feature film that shoots in Philadelphia called *The In Crowd*.

In the middle of all of this Bill gets sober. On his suggestion I start attending Al-Anon meetings. Even then, every time I see him or talk to him I still believe we are destined to be together. I make it a point to stress how great I am doing whenever we rendezvous so he will think I have it together and want me back.

When *The In Crowd* wraps, the production company offers me a job in Los Angeles.

Charles shows up at my apartment in a suit and tie, a bouquet of flowers in his hand. He asks me to marry him. I turn him down. Our loneliness will not disappear if we marry each other. We are the very best of friends, not lovers. He is upset when I take the job in LA, sublet my New York City apartment, and move to the west coast.

1987: The LA job is not what I expected it to be. LA is remote and depressing and I miss theatre. I go back to voice lessons and auditions.

1988: I quit the job that brought me to LA and find a number of part-time jobs—I am a masseuse in a health club, a television actress's personal assistant, a hostess at a restaurant.

1989: I am about to call Bill up and demand we stop this charade and admit our love for each other when my phone rings. Our mutual friend Billy is on the line with news. Bill has just married someone else.

On the Fourth of July, Charles, my soul mate and the man who loved me like no other, dies of AIDS in New York City.

And never another word written.

17

UNMASKED

AND NEVER ANOTHER WORD WRITTEN.

After I relocated to Los Angeles in 1986, I returned to New York City as often as I could. I missed the city and my family and Charles. On one visit, in 1988, I arranged to meet Charles on the Upper West Side for lunch. As I walked up Broadway to meet him I spotted him on the far corner of the street. He looked gray and thin and I knew immediately he was sick. *Not Charles*, I thought to myself. The loss of so many of my friends and colleagues to AIDS had been calamitous. Charles had been spared, I thought. The sight of him pale and fragile made me sick with anger. *No. Not Charles.*

Charles had AIDS. There was no cure. I could do very little for him living so far away. We spoke on the phone as often as we could, frustration in our voices at the useless words that did not come close to expressing what we were truly feeling and really wanted to say. One day I demanded Charles move to Los Angles so that I could take care of him. He thanked me and explained why it was a very bad idea. Nothing we did would change what was coming.

In the end, the best way we communicated was via letters full of pledges of love meant to ensure that the other fully understood our devotion to each other, in case we did not get another chance to elaborate. *I love you. I thank you for your love. I will always be with you, even if I am no longer here.*

As Charles grew weaker, volunteers from his church moved into his apartment and set up a hospice for him. On the Fourth of July weekend of 1989, I flew to New York. At this point, Charles had been bedridden for some time. The virus had attacked his eyes and brain and he could no longer see. He was experiencing bouts of dementia. I arrived on July 3, and the caregiver on duty disappeared to run some errands. I sat down in a chair next to the bed and grabbed Charles's hand. He turned his head to me and quoted from *Coal Miner's Daughter*: "I want you to look to the heavens, Loretta." Then he began to laugh. I picked up his guitar and we sang every country song we knew, our voices blending together for hours, just like old times.

As the sun went down, a sound of popping firecrackers drifted in through the open windows in Charles's apartment. In the late afternoon I prepared to leave. I told Charles I was taking the train to Long Island, but would return in a few days. "It's too noisy to die," he said to me before I walked through his bedroom doors for the last time.

On July 4, with my sister and nephew, I watched the Southampton parade march down Main Street. I cannot remember how I found out Charles died but he did, at 9:15 a.m., after all his visitors had gone and there was only one volunteer left by his side. He was forty years old.

At his funeral his spirit entered my body and took over. The most profound sensation of utter calm enveloped me for a full five minutes. I have never experienced a sensation like it before or since. It was as if Charles had chosen to share with me where he was. It was so beautiful, such a pervasion of love that, at first, I was afraid to let it in. When I did, I held onto it as long as I could before I let it go.

After he died I remembered a conversation we had right after he was diagnosed where he reminded me life was for the living. "Live," he instructed me. How could I live without him? I looked around and saw nothing left to live for. I had given the best parts of myself away.

Even though courage and strength were gifted to me, by birth, by my parents, by some divine being, I lost the ability to forgive myself. I defined myself by my relationship to others: movie star's girlfriend, formerly battered woman, heroine savior of women in theatre. All the potential for a brilliant life vanished when, at the age of twenty-three, I moved to New York City, got a job waiting tables in Greenwich Village, and put my life on hold. How could I have messed up so much?

For a long, long time I did not stop thinking, *what if, what if, what if.*

What if I never met Bill? I would have become a success.

What if I had not been battered? I would have become a success.

What if I had not spent so much time as an advocate for other artists? I would have become a success.

I missed out on becoming the person I should have become. This permeated my thoughts every day, consuming me with regret for the one very wrong choice that resulted in a life lived in fear of making more mistakes.

I waited and waited and waited to make a lot of money, garner recognition, and be an artist. Until my artistic output was heard, seen, experienced by many, I was a failure. I believed that fame was the only measure of my talent. Until I achieved it, I remained a nameless nobody.

Aphra Behn saved me. Creative and funny, strong and intrepid, Aphra Behn fearlessly co-opted a name and an identity and ventured out to create change. Aphra Behn made mistakes, forgave herself, and moved on. Aphra Behn was a success because her gorilla mask protected her from ever measuring herself against the world.

Success. What is it, really, but the ability to crawl out of the era of low self esteem and never go back.

Getting cast in a theatre production or a movie or having my play produced does not make me an artist. Art is in me, lives in my soul, the vibration inside fights a way out to make stuff up. Nobody has to buy this stuff, this art, or look at it, or produce it. It is art because I am an artist and I made it up. If it is the truest stuff I can make, it is a success.

Not to say that getting money for your art is not okay. It is. But it is no longer the criterion by which I identify myself as an artist.

I have been a woman with no identity and a woman with a fake identity. From nameless girlfriend of somebody famous, to a gorilla-masked activist, I am ready to unmask.

I am Donna Kaz. I am Aphra Behn. I am an artist, an activist, and a survivor. I am gender parity and feminism and humor. I am theatre and I am comedy and I am perfect rhythm and I am talent.

I am success.

I am a success.

With all my secrets revealed I go forward without a barrier between me and the world. I take complete responsibility for every part of my amazing life, everything that has ever happened to me, all of it sewn together now, rough seams and all. The clouds move one way above me and the earth moves another way below me. I am at the center of it all.

My story is at the end of a pencil poised over an empty page.

I picked the pencil up.

And wrote.

18

1990–2012, LOS ANGELES AND NEW YORK CITY

Hello Guerrilla Girls,

I was so . . . so delighted to see the article about you in *Backstage* . . . am broke and barely able to send this e-mail but so glad you are out there . . . maybe keeping the door open and/or encouraging others to write, produce, and respect and change the odds with regard to gender . . . thank you ladies, women, girls . . .

Dear Guerrilla Girls,

Try being a male, white, heterosexual playwright over forty in America today and see just how much power you have. The answer is: none at all. And the grants are all for minorities and for theatres who continue to present the same playwright's work again and again, leaving the NEA or whatever it is called irrelevant. Older white heterosexual male playwrights have no power in theatre whatsoever and I find your gender wars approach to the arts distasteful and ultimately counterproductive. Grow up ladies and stop whining.

Dear Guerrilla Girls,

I have been a big fan of your activity for a while now, and was thrilled to see you highlighted in *Backstage* this week. As a woman playwright, director, performer, and labor union rep, I started giggling (on the job) with glee to see that you are targeting the theatre community as well as the visual art world. Please, please send me any postcards, stickers, etc., and I will GLADLY join in on the distribution.

It takes a few years for the Guerrilla Girls to sort ourselves out, but in the end we agree to form three groups. The Guerrilla Girls theatre committee segues into Guerrilla Girls On Tour! and functions more like an activist theatre company. In the months after September 11, 2001, we decide that part of our mission will be to find out what other feminists are creating, thinking, and facing. We will cross borders, take to the road, travel beyond New York City to learn what it is like for women in the rest of the world. And we will do it by making touring theatre addressing gender parity and other issues like war, human rights, body image, pay equity, and violence against women. We will be inclusive and diverse, but recognize that true equality is our goal. We trade our full-headed rubber masks for wigs and even smaller gorilla masks to smash through the walls that remain between us and the audience.

We will do all of it all with humor, finding our own brand of comedy that is broad and physical, full of slapstick, pies in the face, one-liners, parody, and outrageous happiness. We fully turn feminism into a fantastic spectacle, lob bananas to the audience, and trip over each other to perfect the art of being funny feminists. We continue to make posters.

I ♥ Feminism

MORE THAN EVER

THEN	NOW
Women earn less than men.	Women earn less than men.
Equal Rights Amendment not part of the U.S. constitution.	Equal Rights Amendment not part of the U.S. constitution.
Less than 15% of all U.S. Senators and Representatives are women.	Less than 15% of all U.S. Senators and Representatives are women.

A Public Service Message From

Guerrilla Girls On Tour!

www.guerrillagirlsontour.com • P.O. Box 2100 New York, NY 10021

Fifteen years later, as of this writing, 19.4 percent of the U.S. Congress are women.

1990: I study with legendary acting teacher Sanford Meisner.

I return to Yaddo to work on a new play.

I hear what sounds like a man beating up a woman in the house next to my apartment. I call the police.

1991: My play *The Wanderer* is optioned for a production in Los Angeles.

1992: I answer calls for the LA rape and battery hotline. I am introduced to the neighbor of another volunteer on the hotline. He is from London and makes me laugh. We fall in love and get married. For our honeymoon we go to Paris.

There is still a silence in American theatre. It's not a Pinteresque pause or the dead stillness that happens when an actor forgets his lines. It's the systematic silencing of women's voices.

Women have been writing plays for eleven centuries. Without works by women the theatre canon would be absurdly incomplete.

Across the globe new groups have organized to also address discrimination in theatre—Los Angeles Female Playwrights Initiative, 50/50 in 2020, the Kilroys, the International Centre for Women Playwrights, to name a few. People are talking, but the fact remains it has not gotten much better for women playwrights (and directors, designers, producers, etc.). Discrimination in theatre is still ignored by the theatre community, the audiences, and the funders. In many ways, women playwrights might now be classified alongside bluefin tuna— we are both almost extinct.

In 2012, Guerrilla Girls On Tour! joins forces with many new and old organizations addressing discrimination against women and artists of color in theatre to present our issue on a unified and grander guerrilla scale. On September 24 we come out of the jungle and go straight to the Cherry Lane Theatre to host *We Are Theatre,* a speakout for gender parity in theatre.

We Are Theatre does not happen overnight. For almost one year a small band of like-minded guerrilla theatre activists meets month after month. Munching on fair-trade bananas, we plan an evening of kick-ass plays by women by sending e-mails to women playwrights we know and women playwrights we do not know, with a request they write us a reflective, constructive, personal, experimental, or angry monologue/short play about sexism in theatre. And then we wait.

And wait.

And wait.

Finally, we receive a response from one playwright—a writer of color who had experienced some success (plays produced and published) early in her career. "It disturbs me that I have had such a tentative place at the theatre table," she writes to me. "I have since turned to novels and other artistic expressions."

We are too late. Women playwrights have moved on without anyone noticing. They are writing novels, poems, and essays instead of plays. They are focusing their creativity elsewhere.

The theatre won't die (right away at least) without women playwrights. Plays by men have sustained it and can continue to do so. A world without Shakespeare or David Mamet would be unimaginable to some. But what about a world without Suzan-Lori Parks, Lisa Kron, Sarah Ruhl, Katori Hall, Jeanine Tesori, Quiara Hudes, Annie Baker, Amy Herzog, and all the other women playwrights?

After a month of silence, my in-box slowly begins to be filled with beautiful monologues, scenes, and short plays by women. The women playwrights had put my call to write short works for the speakout on their to-do list, but for whatever reason (time, energy, rage) had postponed sitting down to their desks to write about being in the less-than-20-percent category. Theresa Rebeck, Kate Bornstein, Lauren Ferebee, Brooke Berman, and Shay Youngblood, among others, answer the call with funny, sad, angry works about alienation, extinction, isolation, backlash, absurdity, and tokenism. We hear from quota queens, lesbians, futuristic feministas, transgender activists, and grandmothers who give voice to being less than, mistaken, and forgotten.

On the morning of September 24, I sneak out of my cage at the

Bronx Zoo and make my way down to the Cherry Lane where lights are being focused, microphones are being set up, and a bevy of volunteers are folding programs, and think, *Are we really going to pull this off? For just one night in New York City will discrimination in theatre end? Will production of plays by women rise way above 17 percent, the usual percentage of plays by women produced across the U.S., because of our speakout? Or is this going to be just another bitch fest?*

My thoughts are interrupted by the ringing of my new iPhone. Isadora Duncan is on the other line calling me with news.

— Aphra! The Roundabout Theatre has announced its 2012–13 season!

— Yes? Yes? Spit it out!

— The Roundabout has decided to produce ZERO plays by women and hire NO women directors on their main stage for 2012–13.

— Grrrrrrrrrr!

— That's not all. This is Chicago's Guthrie Theater's fiftieth anniversary and they are celebrating with NO plays by women on their main stage and have hired just one woman director.

— GRRRRRRRRR!!!!

As the performers begin to arrive for a walk-through, I go on my social media sites and send out a call to action to blitz the Roundabout with emails, faxes, phone calls, and more. Go to our web site and download our "In this theatre the taking of photographs, the use of a recording device, and the production of plays by women is strictly prohibited" sticker, I write. And just in case Roundabout Artistic Director Todd Haimes doesn't know any women playwrights, I forward him an invite to the speakout.

When the lights dim that evening I sneak into the packed house and weep, laugh, and applaud with the rest of the crowd for *We Are Theatre*. We are theatre. It is time for the stories of women to be produced on stages across the world. Only when women's narratives are equally heard can solutions rise to some of the injustices that plague us all. Without the voice and the vision of women and artists of color, the theatre is a play without a second act.

19

LOS ANGELES

IT WAS NOT THE SWOLLEN EYE or the scraped cheek or the black-and-blue wrists or the lovemaking after. It was not the bath mat ripped out from under me so violently that I flew into the air and landed hard on my back, breaking a finger and bruising my spine. It was not the *I'm sorry*s strung together like a mantra floating from his ash-pale lips while his limp body curled inside my arms and shook with sadness until the dawn. It was not the complete lack of rest, the life lived on high alert, the darting eyes, the debilitating fear that the very next thing I said would trigger another fall into blackness. It was not the flowers or the brand-new Seiko watch or the fancy dinners out or the love notes tacked up all over the house that I suspected were only a pause, a blip, a temporary reprieve from the brandished butcher knife, broken door, lines of cocaine, and liter after liter of scotch. Nothing was enough to end it. In the end, it was he who left me. Not even the golden days of marathon sex culminating in sweet moments of stillness where he held me while the ocean crashed outside the window and time stopped were enough to make it last.

And there was this: Even though he beat me, I was not battered. I only ended up in the emergency room once, so how bad could it have been? I was not battered like in-the-newspapers battered. Not broken-teeth-fractured-nose-split-lip-shattered-ribs-burn-marked-wrists-à-la-

Hedda-Nussbaum battered. He was a movie star, for Christ's sake, not some low-class loser. Not some strange assailant. This is my truth.

For thirteen years I kept the secret desire that he would realize I was his and he was mine alive in my bloodied and oozing broken heart. No other man was good enough, strong enough, exciting enough, abusive enough. After our three-year, 24/7 affair broke up, we both became involved with other people, but it did not matter. We were kismet, meant to drift back together for the next ten years on our private ocean of love. As our past floated behind us like day-old chum, we remained oblivious to the smell of rot following us wherever we went. After one chance hookup with him at the Hotel Bel-Air or my Upper West Side apartment, I drifted on a cloud for months even though as soon as I blinked he disappeared again.

And then, one sun-filled day exactly like every other sun-filled day in Los Angeles, after I had not heard from him because he had been married to someone else for many months, I was at my desk in my new apartment when an idea unlike any other idea I had ever had came to me.

My sweet landlady, Georgia, had turned the back porch and garage of her split-level home into a secluded one-bedroom apartment with windows on three sides. I hunkered down at my desk with my fresh cup of coffee, watched the sun glide lazily over the green grass, and thought, *So what if I have no money?* I am an artist, still. I am whole and free and inside of me ideas are bubbling. A fit of extreme pleasure overtook me at that moment. And the very next thing that came into my head was that I should do some volunteer work for the local domestic violence hotline.

One Saturday morning soon after, I drove to the downtown offices of the LA Commission on Assaults Against Women to begin LA Rape and Battery Hotline training.

In a two-story building on Wilshire Boulevard I sat on a folding chair in a cramped room with forty other women waiting for the first session to begin. We each held in our hands stacks of folders of information and schedules we had been given. The meeting began with a short welcome from Patti Giggans, LACAAW's director, and one by one we went around and introduced ourselves.

— I'm Ellen. I am a rape survivor.

— I'm Sue. Survivor, domestic violence.

— I'm Carol, survivor.

Survivor, survivor, survivor. Wait a second. Survivor? The word rang in my ears. I repeated it to myself, closed my eyes, and saw the letters swirl around as I mouthed the syllables.

Survivor.

I am being dragged by the feet along the hallway. I am gripping the dashboard of the rental car as it skids wide across the road. I am waking up on the floor with a nosebleed.

Survivor, survivor, survivor. The women in the row in front of me drone on, their words bounce off the walls and back into my ears.

There is a door torn from its hinges and a shower curtain ripped from the bar. There is a broken bottle of aspirin on the living room floor. Behind a door a whimpering dog is tied up inside a pitch-black garage.

Now the floodgates of memory crash open wide and spill.

— If you tell anyone, I will kill you.

But I did not tell anyone. Ever. Ever.

A pillow pressed into my face, smothering me. I gasp for air.

And suddenly the truth is a swarm of gnats buzzing around my ears I cannot swat away. The truth is a fact come home. The truth is a flasher clomping down the hallway, unloosening the belt on his trench coat, whipping it open and exposing everything, his tongue slack on his chin, a drop of spit sliding down his lip before it plops off and onto the floor.

And. I. Am. Sick.

I want to fall off the earth and float away, but here I am, in the safest place I could ever possibly be, a haven where every past experience and all that comes with it can be sheltered. Everything save the shame.

I choke back the bile of denial I have been swallowing for years, run out of the room toward I do not know what, turn right, and fall to my knees. Very quickly two counselors are by my side to ask if I am all right. The only words I can speak are: I am a survivor too.

One of the counselors, Denise, bends down and lays a hand on my back. She tells me it is not uncommon for someone in hotline training to be hit with the truth for the very first time. She reassures me, tells me in a bell-tone voice that that part is over now. Her face is calm, her eyes bright and focused on me as she says you are only as sick as your secrets.

We sit down next to each other, our shoulders touch in the cramped alcove, and for the first time, I tell someone my story of surviving domestic violence.

I complete the hotline training and each week during a four-hour shift I answer hang-ups, crank calls, regulars who need someone to talk to for five minutes, and women with real questions. How can I tell if I am battered? How do I get out? How will I get money to live on if I go? What if he finds me? What about my kids? What about my kids? What about my kids?

(Phone rings)

— Hello?

— (whispering) Can you hear me?

— Yes, I can hear you.

— My boyfriend calls me names all the time. He doesn't hit me, though. Wait. I may have to hang up.

— Is there a number I can call you back?

— He doesn't like me to give out this number. He has a very hard job. He's all stressed out. That's why he yells.

— You can use words to abuse others. It does not have to be physical to be abusive. In case we get disconnected, can I can give you the number of a place to go where you can get—

(*Click*)

I hear my own voice in every call. I dole out facts and phone numbers and words of encouragement and hear my young, ignorant self on

the line. Call the police, I say. Call because I never did. File a restrain-
ing order because I never did. Pack an emergency bag and keep it close
by in case you have to run because I certainly never did. I wonder what
would have happened to me if the car had crashed or the knife had
slipped or the police had shown up. *Here is your one chance,* I repeat on
the hotline, *a chance I never took, so take it for me and get the hell out right
now.*

Amid all this reclaiming of my past there is still this: part of me
feels like a big fat faker. What if he finds out what I am saying about
him? It's all lies!

But it is not lies. It is the truth.

Just in case he ever does resurface (the odds are great that he would
one day come back once again), I have a personal manifesto ready for
the next time I see him.

— Oh, hey, how's it going? Long time no see!

— Stop right there and repeat after me: I physically beat and
abused you.

— What?

— You heard me, say it! I physically beat and abused you.

— I'm not going to say that!

— Say, I am a batterer and my behavior was and is unacceptable.

— You're nuts!

— Promise you will help to stop the cycle of violence.

— What's gotten into you?!

— Vow to step aside and allow me to follow my chosen career path
even it if means you must sacrifice your own career so mine might
flourish.

— Boy, have you changed.

Changed in some ways, but in others exactly the same. The dreams
I had of being an actor, a dancer, a director, a producer, a painter, a
writer have not quite been beaten out of me. I have been coaxed back
to LA by a job and work for a film production company. As I bounce
around from script reader to assistant director, my freelance jobs are

semi-creative. In my free time I press on, writing plays and poetry, acting in local theatre productions, playing my guitar, singing at benefits.

My past always manages to get in the way. I have gone from a beach house in Malibu to converted garage in Mar Vista. Whatever I am today, a movie star's girlfriend is what I used to be. My past means more to me than my present.

I know this business, I will say to anyone who would listen. I've been on the inside track. I have gone to movie premieres and visited studios and met famous actors and actresses, because for three years I dated the Oscar-winning actor, blah, blah, blah . . . dropping name after name with a smile and seeing the terrified look begin to creep into the eyes of whomever I am talking to. Perhaps they suspect me to be one of those desperate, crazy actresses when in fact that is exactly what I am turning into. Something gnaws at my insides and makes me believe I will never measure up unless I can BE JUST AS SUCCESSFUL AND FAMOUS AS HE IS!

Then, in 1993, I am in a terrible car accident. Hit head-on when a driver runs a red light. I sue, and the twenty-five thousand dollars I receive in settlement money I immediately decide to put into producing a play I have written for myself called *The Wanderer*, a one-act that uses driving the streets of LA (of all things) as a metaphor for a quest to find direction. The play is staged at a small theatre called the Wooden O in Santa Monica just under the 405 freeway.

On June 17, 1994, at 7:55 p.m., five minutes before the curtain goes up, I peek out to see who is in the audience and the theatre is empty. It is the second week into the run and I have been having decent houses. I run backstage, ask the stage manager where everyone is. He tells me they are outside waiting to watch O. J. Simpson's white Ford Bronco pass on the 405.

The previous week, on June 13, Nicole Brown Simpson and Ron Goldman were found murdered in front of Nicole's Brentwood condo. In the days that follow, the news is saturated with images of Nicole Brown Simpson looking fresh and radiant, then looking disheveled, a black eye blooming above a raw red cheekbone. Over and over her calls for help to 911 provide background noise as experts dispense their take on why she stayed in a violent relationship. Four days later, O. J. Simpson leads the LAPD on an hour-long low-speed car chase on the 405 freeway, right beside the theatre I am about to perform in.

As I sit backstage waiting for O. J. Simpson's Bronco to pass, I think about how instead of sitting comfortably in their seats anticipating my performance, my entire audience is standing outside waiting for an asshole to pass by. Someone who beat up and probably killed his wife and her friend is making a break for it and people are pulled toward him as if he is a hero making a triumphant dash for freedom. I am an actor at a tiny theatre in a low-budget production of a small play and I am being upstaged by a famous jerk careening down the freeway overhead.

At 8:10, a mass of sirens screams by as O.J. passes, and my audience files back in. The curtain goes up at 8:15. My entire performance is driven by the overwhelming desire to redirect the focus back toward me. I am just as important—no, I am far more important—than a crime suspect. I take the rage, the sorrow, and the powerlessness I feel about being formerly battered, unsuccessful as an artist, and female and funnel it into the performance of a lifetime.

A few nights later, Patti Giggans of LACAAW comes to the show. After the performance I tell her I would like to talk to her about working at LACAAW full-time. I made up my mind to become an advocate for women in a greater sense. I long to join the front lines and work in the domestic-violence movement.

— No, says Patti.

— What?

— After seeing your play I think this is what you should pursue.

— But . . .

— Listen, maybe you can write a play about violence against women, but this is what you should do. This is how you should address it. Not by working in an office. By writing plays.

. . . write a play about violence against women . . . be an artist and an activist . . . an activist artist . . .

From then on it seems like I have no choice but to follow the direction Patti has pushed me toward. In 1994 I move back to New York City and in 1997 join the Guerrilla Girls. Along with finding an outlet for making socially conscious art and theatre, I steep myself in feminism, which I believe will eradicate any traces of low self-esteem, rid me forever of longing to go backward in time, and show my batterer I would make it in this world without him.

Yes, feminism will be the antidote to all of my problems.

Before I leave for New York City, Patti asks me to do one last thing for LACAAW.

— What is it?

— The press needs someone to speak about Nicole Brown Simpson. Someone with a similar experience. It won't be easy. You don't have to name any names but you should say no if that's what your gut tells you to do. Think about it and let me know.

And just at that moment another idea unlike any other idea pops into my head. If I stand up in public and speak for Nicole my famous batterer will see it. He will be channel surfing one night in his hotel room while on location somewhere shooting his latest picture and my face will appear on the screen talking about how I had survived him and he will click the pause button, pick up the phone to dial his agent, perhaps stop and think better of it, and at that precise moment my love, my somebody, my assailant, will be gone from my life for good and I will never, ever, ever see him again.

— I don't have to think about it, Patti, I replied. I don't have to think about it at all.

AFTERWORD

NATIONAL DOMESTIC VIOLENCE HOTLINE: 1-800-799-7233 OR TTY 1-800-787-3224

↯

You Are Theatre: *Open up the listings of theatre productions in your local newspaper or Google search it on your computer and count how many of the plays or musicals currently showing are written by women or people of color. Count how many are directed by women or directors of color. Count how many on the creative teams of these productions are women or artists of color. Call, write, or use social media to pressure sexist and/or discriminating theatre companies to produce plays by women and writers of color and to hire more women and artists of color on all their productions. When you go to a sexist theatre, sticker the toilet stalls or rip out the gorilla mask on the next page, cut it out, and wear it in protest during one of their shows.*

LORRAINE
Women buy over 50 percent of the tickets to theatre!

HALLIE
Women make up 52 percent of the population!

APHRA

When will women be better represented in theatre?

ALL

When women want them to be!

APHRA

So go to your local theatre, and if they aren't producing women, turn in your subscriptions.

LORRAINE

Call up the artistic directors and producers and ask them why they don't produce more plays and musicals by women.

HALLIE

And if there is a show by a woman playwright in your town . . .

ALL

BUY A TICKET![23]

---

23 From "The History of Women in American Theatre," by Aphra Behn and Lorraine Hansberry, 2001.

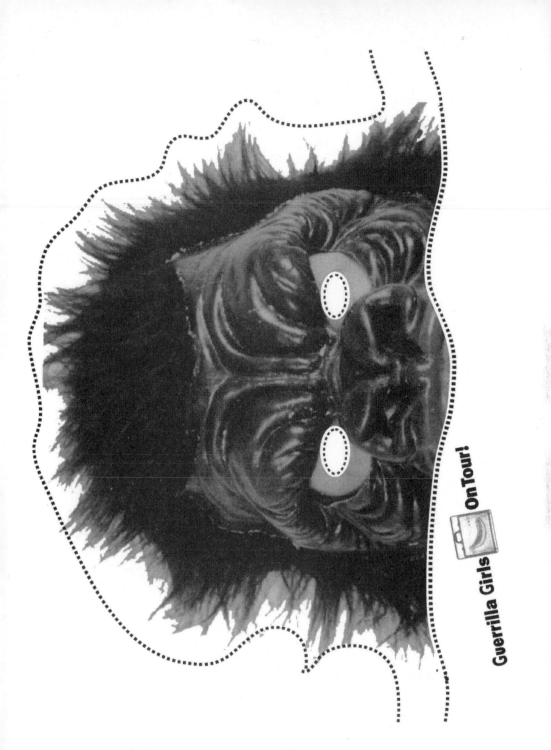

Guerrilla Girls OnTour!

Your Gorilla half mask! Instructions: Rip out, cut out mask/eye holes, attach string to the sides.

ACKNOWLEDGMENTS

HEARTFELT THANKS TO THE MESA REFUGE, the Elizabeth George Foundation, Peace Over Violence, Lit Camp, the Op-Ed Project, EVF Book Club, Alpha Krappy Grammar, American Renaissance Theater Company, Frank Weimann, Alex Hess, Charles T. Harper, Suzannah Lessard, Kathryn Rhett, Natalie Kusz, Peter Stitt, Khris Baxter, Jim McKean, Patti Giggans, Janis Cooke Newman, Mardi Jo Link, Michael Brantley, Tom Conlan, Katie Ornstein, Martha Joy Rose, Daniela Kuper, Chance Parker, Tara Rubin, Laura Henry, Sonia Agron, Terri Muuss, Jennifer Edwards, Martha Wilson, Eric Rayman, Michelle Blankenship, Lyn Hughes, Jody Formica, Mark Lerner, Jim Gunther, Jamie Cherry, Cam Richards, Jennifer Costello, Jennifer Prescott, Carol Bradley, Larry Silver, Bill Vericker, Cathy Roy, Beverly Frank, Gerald Stockstill, Mary Stewart Hammond, Hershall Cook, Debra Stevens, Angelina Fiordellisi, Kym Eisner, Yoko Ono, Jordan Koluch; Deb Di Gregorio, Blue Mountain Center; the Guerrilla Girls, especially Gertrude Stein, Lorraine Hansberry, and Hallie Flanagan; Guerrilla Girls On Tour!: Gracie Allen, Bea Arthur, Josephine Baker, Lili Boulanger, Fanny Brice, Coco Chanel, Julia Child, Alice Childress, Liz Claiborne, Cheryl Crawford, Maya Deren, Isadora Duncan, Edith Evans, Alexandra Exter, Emma Goldman, Frances Harper, Edith Head, Audrey Hepburn, Laura Keene, Eva Le Gallienne, Carole Lombard,

Lisa "Left Eye" Lopes, Fanny Mendelssohn, Edna St. Vincent Millay, Dorothy Parker, Edith Piaf, Anne Sexton, Sophie Treadwell, Lupe Velez, Azucena Villaflor and Anna May Wong; the Art Cheerleaders, my extended Charkham family, every one of my CrossFit coaches and teammates, Wooly, Midge, all the people I worked with at Jimmy Day's and the Saloon; my classmates at SUNY Brockport.

Lastly, blessings and love to my family for being there from the very beginning: Matka and Pop along with Ray, Ken, Dynie, and their families.

AUTHOR'S NOTE

THIS MEMOIR IS BASED ON THE many personal journals, diaries, and notebooks of writings and drawings I have kept since high school, as well as notes, memos, e-mails, letters, phone calls, and other communications during my time as a Guerrilla Girl and Guerrilla Girl On Tour![24] I have used only the pseudonyms of all Guerrilla Girls and Guerrilla Girls On Tour! Guerrilla Girls, Inc. has not authorized any part of this book.

Dialogue has been reconstructed to the best of my memory. Some names have been changed and in one instance in chapter four, two events were compressed.

Parts of chapter eighteen were previously published in *The Dramatist* in 2013.

---

24 Guerrilla Girls On Tour! (ggontour.com) is a touring theatre company founded in 2001 by Lorraine Hansberry, Aphra Behn, and Hallie Flanagan, former members of the Guerrilla Girls. Guerrilla Girls On Tour! is now a separate organization from the original Guerrilla Girls, and our focus is to develop new and original plays, performances, and workshops that dramatize women's history and advocate on behalf of women and artists of color in the performing arts.

I have written the events in my life exactly as I remember them and have been as truthful as possible. This is my memory of what happened to me.